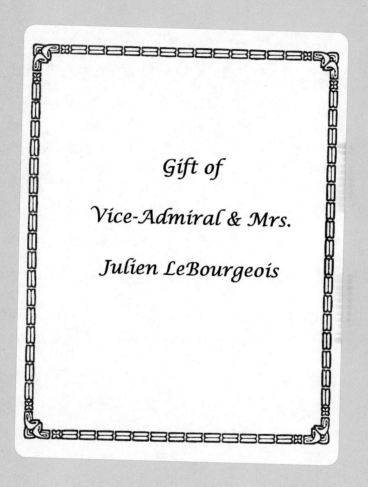

V. SCHWARZ

Leningrad

Art
and
Architecture

PROGRESS PUBLISHERS · MOSCOW

Translated from the Russian by *Olga Shartse*
Designed by *Grigory Dauman*

В. Шварц · ЛЕНИНГРАД

Художественные памятники

На английском языке

First printing 1972

Printed in the Union of Soviet Socialist Republics

Leningrad

One of the Rostral columns

Leningrad, the cradle of the Great October Revolution, well deserves the honour of bearing Lenin's name. Its streets and squares are a live chronicle of glorious deeds: every building here is a memorial, every stone a bit of history. From the Neva, the cruiser *Aurora* fired the shot that gave the signal for attack on the night of October 25th (November 7th) 1917, and the sound called an echo throughout the world. It was here, in Leningrad, that the Soviet Government's first decrees on peace and land were issued.

By request of the working people of Petrograd, the city was renamed Leningrad in January 1924, and this is what was said in the resolution of the Second Congress of Soviets of the U.S.S.R. "Red Petrograd is the cradle of proletarian revolution. The workers of Petrograd have rendered invaluable service to our Union of Soviet Socialist Republics. And it was here in Petrograd that the great events of October 1917 which decided the future of our country took place." The resolution ended with the words: "Hereafter, let this largest centre of proletarian revolution be forever linked with the name of the greatest leader of the proletariat—Vladimir Ilyich Ulyanov (Lenin)."

The city—St. Petersburg—Petrograd—Leningrad—is a little over two-and-a-half centuries old. In the course of its history different foreign invaders made attempts to seize it, but no armed enemy has ever set foot on Leningrad soil. In recognition of the Leningraders' war effort and creative endeavour, their city has been decorated with the Gold Star, two Orders of Lenin, the Order of the October Revolution, and the Order of the Red Banner. It has received the honourable title of hero city together with Moscow, Odessa, Sevastopol, Volgograd and Kiev. Thousands of Leningraders wear the medal "For the Defence of Leningrad" awarded for the unparalleled heroism displayed in the Great Patriotic War.

Leningrad is also one of the Soviet Union's major industrial and cultural centres, and the second largest and most important town in the U.S.S.R. A great variety of machines and apparatus, ranging from unique hydroturbines to the finest of optical precision instruments, are manufactured at Leningrad's famous enterprises, among them the Kirov Works (formerly the Putilov Works), the Twenty-Second Party Congress Metal Works, and the Kirov Electrosila factory. They are shipped to all ends of the Soviet Union and exported to countries abroad.

The five railway stations—Moscow, Vitebsk, Warsaw, Baltic and Finland—seethe with noisy, bustling activity day and night. Ships flying the flags of many countries can be seen in the Leningrad harbour.

One walk through the streets of Leningrad is enough to feel the tense rhythm of big-city life compounded of the businesslike hurry, the streams of traffic, the swinging arms of cranes in the distance, and—in the evening—the blazing neon advertisements, the brightly lit entrances to the theatres, cinemas, clubs, restaurants and cafés, and again the gaily hurrying crowd.

Leningrad's contribution to Russia's culture and art is inestimable. It gave birth and inspiration to many of our great poets, writers, painters, sculptors, composers and actors. Much of the life and work of Pushkin, Lermontov, Gogol, Nekrasov, Belinsky, Chernyshevsky, Glinka, Chaikovsky, Repin, Kramskoi, Shevchenko and Mayakovsky is connected with Leningrad.

The names of Leningrad's leading scientists, writers and actors enjoy world renown. The cultural life of this modern city has a great deal to offer

Monument to V. I. Lenin in front of Smolny

the Leningraders: there are more than 40 educational institutions of the higher level, 2,600 libraries, 19 theatres, over 80 museums and permanent exhibitions, and roughly 130 Houses of Culture and clubs.

The streets, embankments and squares are in themselves works of art created by great masters. One can gaze for hours at the panorama opening from the banks of the Neva: at the Peter and Paul Fortress with its gleaming spire, at the railings of the numerous bridges spanning the beautiful river, at the palaces with their rows of slender columns, and simply at the reflection of all this in the water.

Leningrad is rightly considered one of the most beautiful cities in the world. The buildings and ensembles designed by Rastrelli, Zakharov, Voronikhin, Rossi, Stasov and other eminent masters belong to the best in world architecture. All these buildings are taken good care of by the Soviet state, and where necessary highly skilled restoration work is done on them.

Since the October Revolution dozens of new buildings, streets, squares and parks have appeared in Leningrad, complementing and enhancing its architectural identity.

Large-scale housing development has given the Leningraders new streets of apartment houses and new residential neighbourhoods. This, as elsewhere in the country, is how the socialist town-planning principles based on concern for the population are implemented.

View of the Peter and Paul Fortress from the
spit (Strelka) of Vasilyevsky Island

The city has an area of 53,000 hectares and is built up along the banks of the Neva, its tributaries and arms, and on the 101 islands formed in the delta. On one of the islands in the widest part of the delta stands the Peter and Paul Fortress, its grim stone walls rising high above the water. The foundation stone of the fortress was laid on May 16 (Old Style) 1703, the day St. Petersburg was founded.

The city appeared and began to develop under the protection of the fortress which was Russia's outpost in the Northern War with Sweden.

The lands along the banks of the Neva were the arena of many fierce battles. Again and again, Russian soldiers had to repel the attacks of foreign invaders who were determined to seize the strategically important river mouth which was a convenient outlet to the Baltic Sea. Early in the 17th century these lands were temporarily ceded to the Swedes, but foreign domination could not be long-lived here with Russia's rapid development and her imperative need of a sea gateway. As Karl Marx wrote in his *Secret Diplomacy of the 18th Century:* "No great nation had ever existed or could exist in such remoteness from all seas as Peter the Great's empire was in the beginning ... no great nation had ever reconciled itself to having all its sea shores and river mouths taken away from it. No one could imagine a great nation isolated from the sea shores. Russia could not let the Swedes keep the mouth of the Neva which was a natural outlet for the shipment of goods."

The historical task of restoring the Neva lands to Russia was accomplished by the Russian people in the course of the Northern War (1700—1721).

In 1702—1703 the scene of battle shifted to the banks of the Neva. In October 1702, the Russian army stormed and seized the ancient Oreshek (Hard Nut) fortress (which the Swedes had renamed Noteborg) on the shore of Lake Ladoga, not far from the source of the Neva. Peter the Great ordered the fortress to be thereafter called Schlüsselburg, meaning key-town, thus underlining its key position on the river. Schlüsselburg was later renamed Petrokrepost (Peter's Fortress).

The Nienschantz Fortress, where the Okhta flows into the Neva, was the Swedes' only remaining stronghold on the Neva.

At the end of April 1703, the Russian armies laid siege to this fortress. In the meantime, Peter took several companies of the Preobrazhensky and Semyonovsky Regiments and sailed down the river with the aim of surveying the Neva mouth and occupying it "against enemy invasion from the sea". Apparently it was then that Peter's eye was caught by a small island called Zayachy (Hares') or Vesyoly (Jolly) Island. Situated at the point where the river branched out into two arms, the island made a good defence position: artillery fire from there would bar the way to enemy ships on both the Bolshaya (Big) and the Malaya (Small) Nevas. It was decided to build a new fortress on this island when the war council agreed that it was inexpedient to rehabilitate the Nienschantz fortress after the Russian armies had taken it, to quote from the original document: "for reason of it being small, far removed from the sea, and the site being not too secure by nature."

The foundation stone was laid on May 16 (Old Style) and the fortress was named Saint Petersburg. The ground plan had the outlines of an octagon, adapted to the contours of the island and slightly stretched out between the Neva and the strait which was later named the Kronverksky Strait.

The Neva on a white night

The Peter and Paul Cathedral

Iconostasis in the Peter and Paul Cathedral

Three protruding parts of the wall, known as the bastions, face the Neva, and the three other—the Kronverksky Strait. The earthworks were in the main completed by the end of that same summer of 1703. Peter the Great personally supervised the work on one of the bastions, and his followers Menshikov, Golovkin, Naryshkin, Zotov and Trubetskoi had charge of the other five which bear their names to this day.

The fortress was built under extremely difficult conditions, and the excruciating toil, lack of food, damp and cold took its toll of many lives.

A few years later the earthen walls were replaced with brick fortifications, and towards the end of the 18th century the walls were faced with granite slabs.

On June 29 (Old Style) 1703, the foundations of the Peter and Paul Cathedral, a wooden building, were laid with the attending ceremony. Later, the fortress took its name from the cathedral. Construction of a stone building in place of the wooden one was begun in 1712, to be completed only 21 years later. The architect was Domenico Trezzini, a Swiss who came to work in Russia at the invitation of Peter the Great and found his second home here. Creatively assimilating the traditions and peculiarities of Russian national architecture, Trezzini designed a number of outstanding buildings in St. Petersburg, but his unexcelled masterpiece is the Peter and Paul Cathedral.

The rectangular building is dominated by a tall bell tower crowned with a spire which gleams in a vertical line above the relatively low fortress walls. The belfry, designed in tiers, towers over the western part of the cathedral. From afar the beginning and end of the tiers are almost unnoticeable, and the belfry appears a single whole, logically tapering to a spire. Crowning it is a weathervane in the shape of an angel carrying a cross. The angel looks tiny from below, but in fact it is quite large, measuring 3.2 metres high with a wing span of 3.8 metres.

In his desire to stress the importance of his new city, Peter ordered the belfry with the spire to be taller than the belfry of Ivan the Great in Moscow. His order was obeyed, and the Peter and Paul bell tower measures 122 metres to the tip of the spire (it was 16 metres shorter before reconstruction in the middle of the 18th century) as against Moscow's 79.5 metres. It remained the tallest architectural point in Leningrad until the appearance of the television tower which measures 316 metres.

In those first years, church spires lent beauty and magnificence to the skyline and the general appearance of the town, breaking the monotony of the squat structures built on level ground and uniting them into something like an ensemble. In the 18th century the spire of St. Peter's and St. Paul's Cathedral was struck by lightning several times; in 1756, for instance, it was damaged so badly that it took years to repair it. Even the smallest repairs on the spire called for courage, nimbleness and strength, beside plain skill. The feat performed by Pyotr Telushkin, a roofer, is widely known: in 1830, he managed to climb up to the top of the spire, using only a rope and no scaffolding, and repaired the damaged cross.

The interior of the cathedral is no less interesting. The dominating feature is the carved and gilded wooden iconostasis. The carving was executed by two Moscow masters Trifon Ivanov and Ivan Telega, and the design was made by Ivan Zarudny, a wonderful Russian architect who built the Menshikov Tower in Moscow. The perfection of the filigree work makes one think of dozens of carvers toiling for many long years, but amazingly the two of them—Ivanov and Telega—managed this intricate job in four.

Domenico Trezzini also designed St. Peter's Gate which was originally built of wood and later, in 1717–1718, of stone. This structure—one of the few buildings in the fortress—has remained practically unchanged since it was first built. The entrance arch, which seems very small in comparison to the rest of the structure, is adorned with a double eagle.

In the gate above it there is a large wooden haut relief by Konrad Osner portraying Apostle Peter and Simon Magus. The panels on either side of it, over the side volutes, are decorated with armour, also in haut relief. Decorative statues adorn the niches under these panels. St. Peter's Gate stands out among the other early 18th century structures because of its abundance of sculptural ornaments and its general look of splendour.

In the 18th–19th centuries the architectural ensemble of the Peter and Paul Fortress had other buildings added to it. The "House of the Grandfather of the Russian Navy" where Peter the Great's boat was to be kept was built next to the cathedral in 1761–1762 by architect A. F. Vist. The

St. Peter's Gate

The entrance gate of the Peter and Paul Fortress

Nevsky Gate was reconstructed by architect N. A. Lvov in 1787. And then the Mint was built in 1796–1806, whose design is attributed to architect A. Porto.

The fortress built to protect the Neva banks from possible Swedish invasion, soon lost its defence importance. In 1704, work began on the construction of the Kronstadt Fortress on Kotlin Island which securely barred the enemy fleet's entrance to the mouth of the Neva. Moreover, the victories scored by the Russian armies finally ensured the safety of the Gulf of Finland shores and the Neva country.

In 1717 the Peter and Paul Fortress was turned into a political prison. Prince Alexei, the heir apparent, around whom the opponents to Peter the Great's reforms were grouping themselves, was shortly afterwards confined in the fortress.

I. T. Pososhkov, a prominent economist and publicist, the author of *A Book About Poverty and Richness*—a progressive treatise for the time—ended his life in one of the cells in 1726.

The names of many dedicated revolutionaries will be found in the long lists of prisoners. One is Alexander Radishchev, the great revolutionary democrat who almost paid with his life for his brilliant book *A Journey From St. Petersburg to Moscow* in which he exposed autocracy and serfdom. In July 1826, five leaders of the Decembrists' uprising—K. F. Ryleyev, P. I. Pestel, P. G. Kakhovsky, M. P. Bestuzhev-Ryumin and S. I. Muravyov-Apostol—were executed on the crown work outside the fortress walls. (More about the Decembrists' uprising will be found on page 108).

Nikolai Chernyshevsky, a revolutionary democrat and author of *What Is To Be Done?*, spent long months in solitary confinement in one of the fortress cells. Lenin's elder brother, Alexander Ulyanov, who was one of those who organised the attempted assassination of Alexander III, was confined in the fortress and taken from there to his execution in Schlüsselburg. In January 1905, Maxim Gorky was sentenced to imprisonment in the Trubetskoi Bastion for writing a revolutionary proclamation which called for the overthrow of the monarchy. Lenin's associates N. E. Bauman, P. N. Lepeshinsky and other Bolsheviks had also been kept prisoner in the fortress.

The prison cells were cold and dark like tombs. The conditions and the treatment given the prisoners here had to break their spirit, and undermine their moral and physical strength. Indeed, some men did break down under the strain, and were transferred from the prison to the madhouse. However, most of the political prisoners were made of stronger stuff. As a rule, the revolutionaries manfully endured their solitary confinement, and those who got out alive took up their struggle against the autocracy with redoubled energy.

The Peter and Paul Fortress also figures in the history of the October Revolution. On October 24, when the uprising against the bourgeois Provisional Government began, the garrison of the fortress went over to the side of the revolution. It was from the fortress that the military operations against the Winter Palace—that last stronghold of the Provisional Government—were guided. When the revolutionary workers, soldiers and sailors began to storm the Palace they were supported by gunfire from the fortress. The last prisoners to be confined in its cells were the Ministers of the Provisional Government.

Since 1923, the Peter and Paul Fortress has been a historical museum.

True to an old, and now revived tradition a cannon is fired from the Naryshkin Bastion at noon sharp every day, giving the exact time by which all the Leningraders set their watches.

On holidays, guns are ranged along the walls of the fortress to give the traditional salute. Huge crowds gather on the embankments and the bridges to watch the fireworks which, reflected in the water, makes an unforgettable, colourful spectacle.

Zayachy Island, on which the fortress is situated, is divided from the oldest part of town called Petrogradskaya Storona (Petrograd Side) by the not very wide Kronverksky Strait.

Peter the Great's cottage, built for him on the bank of the Neva, when the city was being founded, still survives. It is a long house no different from ordinary peasant cottages, with an entry and two small rooms. Originally the walls were painted to resemble brick, and the roof was adorned with a painted wooden mortar and wooden shells with "flames of fire" at the ends. Later, a stone shelter was built for the cottage to ensure its preservation. A small bust of Peter the Great was set up in front of it at the end of the 19th century.

In 1907, Manchurian stone Shih Tzes—mythological lion-frog creatures— were erected on the embankment in front of the cottage.

The city's first streets appeared in the vicinity of the Peter and Paul Fortress and Peter's cottage. Originally they were called after skills and estates.

With every year the contrast between the splendour of the palatial buildings on the riverside and the wretchedness of the city builders' dwellings became more glaring. These huts steadily increased in number as more people were needed to cope with the expanding construction. As many as forty thousand serfs were delivered to St. Petersburg from all ends of the country every year. Hundreds of thousands of people, toiling in the sweat of their brow, built up the magnificent city with fantastic speed.

The development of St. Petersburg became especially rapid after the threat of Swedish invasion had been eliminated. In 1710, the Russian armies took Vyborg, which Peter the Great called St. Petersburg's "solid bolster," and when, in 1714, the Swedish navy was routed at Cape Hangö, the security of the young city was finally assured.

St. Petersburg became the capital of Russia in 1713.

In the first ten years of the city's existence when Gorodskoy Island was built up in the main, important construction went on on the other islands as well. A little further downstream from Zayachy Island, on the left bank of the Neva, work began on the Admiralty fortress and wharf in 1704. A large space was cleared for the tsar's summer residence across the river from his cottage. This area was developed to make the Summer Garden, and here—at the point where the Fontanka, then called Bezymyanny Yerik (Nameless Creek), flows into the Neva, Domenico Trezzini built the Summer Palace (1710—1711). It little resembles a palace as one usually imagines it. This is an ordinary two-storey stone house with a tall roof—the original tiles were later replaced with iron—and it looked much like the other houses built at the time by the wealthier residents. At first, the Summer Palace was surrounded by water on three sides. Since there was no embankment yet, the Neva and the Fontanka actually washed its walls.

A small landing stage was built on the southern side with steps running down from the house to the river.

The façade of the palace is simple to the extreme. Originally, its only modest adornment were the platbands around the windows and the rustic masonry at the corners. At a later date, 29 terracotta panels were inserted between the windows of the first and second floors depicting haut-relief

The pavilion inside the Peter and Paul Fortress
where Peter the Great's boat is kept

scenes from ancient mythology, allegorically referring to the Northern War. For instance, one of the panels on the western façade shows Perseus rescuing Andromeda. Here, Perseus personifies Russia, Andromeda—the Izhora country, and the Dragon—Sweden. Or, to put it plainly, the liberation of the Izhora lands and their restoration to Russia.

The lay-out of the first and second floors is absolutely identical: six rooms, kitchen, corridor, and a room for the batmen or ladies-in-waiting on duty. The tsar had the first floor, and the tsarina the second.

Like Peter the Great's cottage, the Summer Palace has been made into a museum. Although not all of its interior decorations and furnishings have been preserved, in general appearance the palace has retained many of its original features.

The Summer Garden is the oldest in Leningrad, existing since 1704. It has an area of a little over 11 hectares. The planning was done by Peter the Great himself who wanted to have a better garden than the French king had in Versailles. Rare trees and flowers were brought in from different parts of Russia and also from Holland, and the best gardeners were mobilised. The garden grew and expanded very quickly. With its precise arrangement, straight walks and neatly trimmed trees and shrubs it was a model formal garden, and the style became very fashionable with the owners of country seats and large estates in the first half of the 18th century. The garden's decorative features included more than fifty fountains, in many of which the themes of Aesop's fables were used, a greenhouse built of stone, oakwood galleries, an aviary where rare birds were kept, a magnificent grotto, and so forth. The Ligovsky Canal was built to channel water for the fountains from the Liga, and three water towers were erected on the Fontanka which is why it was renamed Fontanka (a derivative from the word fountain).

Much of the work in the Summer Garden was done by Jean Baptiste Leblond, a French architect invited to Russia by Peter the Great, two Russian architects M. Zemtsov and I. Matveyev, and gardeners J. Roosen, I. Surmin, L. Lukyanov and I. Yakovlev.

Early in the 18th century, marble statuary began to appear in the garden. Most of the statues were made by Italian sculptors of the Venetian

Shih Tzes in front of Peter the Great's Cottage

Peter the Great's Summer Palace

The study in Peter the Great's Summer Palace

school: Pietro Baratta, Antonio Tarsia, Giovanni Bonazza and others. Some were sculptural portraits, and the busts of Alexander the Great, Julius Caesar, Augustus, Nero, Trajan, Claudius, John the Third of Poland, and Queen Christine, have survived. But the majority of the statues were allegorical, symbolising Truth, Beauty, Honour, Justice, periods of the day, and so on. One of the most interesting sculptural groups stands in front of the Palace's southern façade: this is called "Peace and Abundance" (sculptor Baratta), an allegorical interpretation of the Nieschtadt Peace concluded after Russia's victory in the Northern War. The seated figure holding a cornucopia in her left hand personifies Russia, and the downthrust torch in her right hand symbolises the end of hostilities. The Goddess of Victory, who stands beside her, is crowning Russia with a laurel wreath while trampling underfoot a dying lion—the symbol of conquered Sweden.

Eighteenth century artists often used allegory and rendered the most stirring themes of the day in abstract images. The statuary in the Summer Garden is a good example to the point.

In 1771–1784 a tall grille of cast iron, presumably designed by architects G. Veldten and P. Y. Yegorov, was put up along the riverside frontage of the garden. This grille, made at the Tula Works, is one of the finest adornments of the Neva embankment. There are thirty six pink granite columns, alternately crowned with vases and urns, and the grille between them takes the shape of vertically placed spears, joined by elongated rectangles with wrought iron rosettes in the centre. These rosettes, the ornament, the tips of the spears and the handles of the vases and urns are gilded. The two gates (there used to be three) have a somewhat more intricate design with inset gilded vases and volute ornaments on the top.

Little by little this oldest garden in St. Petersburg changed in appearance. After the flood of 1777 it lost its fountains and its formal character. New structures appeared in the course of time. One was the "Coffee House" designed by Rossi as a one-storey building with a spherical dome, built in 1826 on the site of the demolished grotto. The façade of the house has a raised ornament designed by sculptor V. I. Demut-Malinovsky. The "Tea House" appeared that same year, built by architect L. I. Charlemagne who also designed the grille along the southern boundary of the garden. A large porphyry vase was set up in front of the ancient Karpiyev Pond in the southern part of the garden in 1839. And then, in 1855, a bronze monument to the great Russian fabulist Ivan Krylov (by sculptor P. K. Klodt) was unveiled in the space between the "Tea House" and the main alley. The figure is seated on a 3.5 m high pedestal in a relaxed slightly tired pose. There is nothing spectacular in Krylov's attitude or clothes, it is an informal and not a "posed" portrait. His face and his whole figure are full of a dignified composure. The pedestal is decorated with the characters from Krylov's famous fables, "The Fox and the Sour Grapes," "The Crow and the Fox," "Quartet" and others, done in haut relief to drawings by A. A. Agin.

Not just the appearance but also the role played by the Summer Garden in the life of the city changed with time. In the reign of Peter the Great it was a very exclusive place, and only the courtiers and the most eminent citizens were admitted to the gala celebrations and festivities. As a rule there was a fireworks display with thousands of coloured lights shooting up into the gloomy Petersburgian sky. The displays were at their most magnificent on victory days.

From about the middle of the 18th century, the Summer Garden became open to members of the privileged classes who liked to take their walks there. With the years, this circle widened, and in the early 19th century the garden became very popular with poets, writers, composers and artists. Alexander Pushkin, who lived in Panteleimonovskaya Street adjoining the Summer Garden, wrote in one of the letters to his wife: "It's my kitchen garden. As soon as I get up in the morning I go there in my dressing gown and slippers. After dinner I sleep there, read or write." Taras Shevchenko, the Ukrainian poet and artist, recalled: "In the summer during the white nights I often ran to the Summer Garden to draw the statues."

During the Great Patriotic War (1941—1945) much damage was done to the trees; trenches and foxholes were dug in the lawns; the marble statues were taken down and buried in the ground for safety. Soon after victory, however, the garden recovered its former look thanks to the efforts

Summer Garden

A path in the Summer Garden

of the citizens themselves. Leningraders take good care of their garden: they plant new trees and flowers every year, and keep the historical structures in good repair. In summer and autumn, when the weather is fair, there are always crowds of children playing in front of Krylov's monument, people reading, playing chess in the shade of the ancient trees, or just strolling about till late at night.

Credit for designing the Summer Palace and Garden, the Peter and Paul Fortress and other major early 18th century buildings goes to both Russian and foreign architects. The latter came to Russia from different countries, attracted by the tremendous opportunities offered by the scale on which the building of St. Petersburg was launched. Some of them simply came to make easy money, and some did not stay long enough to accomplish anything worthwhile. But there were people like Domenico Trezzini, for instance, whose name will be forever linked with the early architecture of the city. Failure awaited the foreign master who did not give sufficient thought to the national character of Russian architecture, to the peculiarities of the site and the identity of St. Petersburg. This happened to architect Leblond and the plan of the city which he drew up in 1716–1717 for Peter the Great.

Leblond suggested a rectangular system of streets encircled with fortresses in an ellipse. The city's centre was to be on Vasilyevsky Island, one of the largest islands in the delta of the Neva where it branches into two arms, the Bolshaya and the Malaya Nevas. Leblond proposed crisscrossing the island with canals along which the streets would be laid.

Attempts were made to implement the plan but very soon it became obvious that this was an abstract, unfeasible project. Too much had been left out of account. For one thing, Leblond ignored the fact that St. Petersburg's centre was already shaping along the banks of the Neva, and so the idea of shifting it to the island ran counter to the natural tendency of the city's development. For another, there being no bridges across the Neva, connection with the island presented a problem, and this Leblond did not take into account either.

Although his plan was declined it undoubtedly gave an impetus to the

Aurora (Summer Garden)   Apollo (Summer Garden)

Ceres (Summer Garden)   Pomona (Summer Garden)

development of Vasilyevsky Island in the seventeen-twenties and seventeen-thirties. Another, and even more important impetus, was the transference of the port to the island after Russia's naval victories over the Swedes. More early eighteenth century buildings have survived here than anywhere else. The oldest of these is the Menshikov Palace.

Alexander Menshikov was the first governor-general of St. Petersburg, and Peter the Great made him a gift of the whole island. A great country estate grew up in a short space of time: there was the mansion, a chapel, formal gardens, windmills, storehouses and other such premises. It must be said, that, if anything, St. Petersburg's growth was hindered by these enormous private estates which occupied vast areas and made connection between the different parts of the city difficult to achieve.

The palace—a modest, not very large house is not eye-catching at all, and does not stand out among the other buildings there. The three-storey red-and-white façade is decorated with pilasters, plain platbands, and a pediment in the centre, bearing the date 1710 when construction was begun by Giovanni Maria Fontana who designed the palace. The work was completed in 1716 by G. Schedel.

Originally, the house was more ornate. All the three storeys of the façade had pilasters, there was an attic with a statue on it above the central part of the building, the risalitos were adorned with princely crowns, there was plenty of gilding, and a granite stairway led down to the water. Menshikov's Palace was much larger and much more sumptuously appointed than the tsar's own apartments, and so it was here that foreign ambassadors were received and ceremonious "assemblies" were held.

When Menshikov fell into disgrace, the palace was given over to the Cadet Corps to be used as a military college. This, naturally, called for various changes and additions, notable among which is the long red-and-white building where the First All-Russia Congress of Soviets was convened. At the session held on June 4th (17th) 1917, when one of the speakers said that in Russia there was no political party that could assume power and govern the country, Lenin called out: "There is such a party!" Later that same day Lenin spoke on the attitude to the Provisional Gov-

The grille of the Summer Garden

The entrance gate of the Summer Garden

ernment, and on June 9th (22nd)–against the continuation of the war. The street where this building stands has been renamed the Syezdovskaya Liniya (Congress Line).

Another early eighteenth century building that has survived is the Kikiny Palaty (Mansion)–a large, palace-type building to the west of the Smolny along the Neva. The Mansion was practically destroyed in the Second World War, but its near-original appearance has now been restored to it.

Needless to say, neither Menshikov's Palace nor the Kikiny Palaty belonged to the usual type of dwellings erected early in the eighteenth century, which were incomparably simpler and less ambitious. A special "Building Office" headed by Ulyan Sinyavin, one of Peter the Great's gifted and energetic supporters, was set up in 1709, to deal with the task of building up the town. The Office commissioned Trezzini to design "model" houses for different sections of the population. These houses were to line the long, straight streets of St. Petersburg. While differing in size and in costliness of finish, these "model" houses had to answer certain common stipulations: the layout of the house itself and the adjoining lot had to be kept strictly according to pattern, and the main façade had to face the street, and not away from it as was customary in the preceding period.

The first houses were mainly timber and partly mud, but before long brick began to prevail. Erecting timber houses in the centre of the city, and especially on the banks of the Neva, was prohibited by law. In order to attract all the master-masons to the growing town, Peter issued an *ukase* in 1714 forbidding the erection of stone buildings anywhere else in Russia. Every barge or cart arriving at St. Petersburg had to unload a prescribed number of stones in front of the city gates: otherwise they were refused admittance.

In the early eighteenth century large cities, and European capitals too, were as a rule built up chaotically, but St. Petersburg, growing up in its own planned fashion, assumed the features of a formal city of a neyw type from the very start. This was achieved by setting up the "Building Office", by approving Leblond's plan, and by exercising rigid control over

"Coffee House" in the Summer Garden

Monument to Ivan Krylov

the housing development. A striving for efficient organisation might aptly characterise the general appearance of St. Petersburg in the early eighteenth century.

Structures of a completely novel type also made their appearance in those years: model administrative buildings, production workshops, various fortifications, shipyards, and so forth.

Of the major public buildings on Vasilyevsky Island, two have survived: these are the Kunstkammer and the Twelve Collegia.

The Kunstkammer was designed by architect Georg Johann Mattarnovi who began building it in 1718; the work was continued by N. Gerbel and Gaetano Chiaveri, and completed in 1734 by M. G. Zemtsov. The long frontage is divided into three sections: a tiered, octahedral tower crowned with a spherical dome in the middle, and two identical façades flanking it. The white piedroits, panels and window platbands break the monotony of the walls without, however, interfering with the general impression of formality and reserve. In the past, the risalitos of the side buildings had figured pediments which made them much more attractive. The tiered tower, which is rather complex in composition, is strikingly picturesque. The alternating concave and convex facets of the octahedron are sharply contrasted by the straight lines of the side sections. The first tier rising above the main bulk of the building is also curious in outline. The one on top of it is a regular octahedron with semicircular windows and a balustrade. Above it rises the octahedral turret which supports the spherical dome that crowns the whole composition. The Kunstkammer has many features reminiscent of the picturesque architecture popular in seventeenth-century Moscow.

It was one of the first buildings in Russia specially designed for the use of scientific institutions. It housed the first public museum with its collection of rarities and curiosities, the first library and observatory, and also—until the end of the eighteenth century—the Russian Academy of Sciences, founded by Peter the Great in 1725. A memorial plaque above the central window of the first floor reminds us that Mikhail Lomonosov, the great Russian scientist, had worked here from 1741 to 1765. In the central part of the building there is Lomonosov's Museum. The confer-

View of University Embankment

ence hall where the Academy of Sciences had its meetings, attended by Lomonosov, has been fully restored.

The side sections are occupied by the Museum of Anthropology and Ethnography of the U.S.S.R. Academy of Sciences whose collections illustrate the origin of man, and the life and culture of the nations of the world.

In 1747, a fire broke out in the building, causing it great damage. It was restored except for the turret, and this is how it remained for two hundred years until 1949 when the turret was finally put back in place.

Almost next door to the Kunstkammer, also on the bank of the Neva, stands the Leningrad University, originally called the Twelve Collegia and built by Trezzini in 1722–1741 for Peter the Great's collegia, or the supreme government bodies that were eventually to develop into Ministries. The building faces the Mendeleyevskaya Liniya (Mendeleyev Line), a

Menshikov Palace

Menshikov Palace. Tiled stove

The former Kikin Mansion

Anthropological and Ethnographical Museum of the USSR and the Lomonosov Museum (formerly the Kunstkammer)

Ethnographical Museum

boulevard laid out in recent years where there was once a small canal and a square, and only its side façade is turned to the Neva. Stretching inland for close on five hundred metres, the building is made up of twelve exactly similar parts, each of which has its own roof, its architectural centre, and (in the 18th century) its own entrance. Trezzini's idea was to underline the relative independence of each of the twelve collegia on the one hand, and their close interconnection in the system of state administration, on the other.

The first storey, done in rustic masonry, has large semicircular windows; the second and third storeys are decorated with pilasters, simple panels and window platbands. Each of the twelve sections has a projecting central part with a balcony on the second floor, and a figured pediment. The impression of elegant efficiency is enhanced by the rhythmical repetition of the red-and-white pattern along the length of the whole façade.

In the eighteen-thirties, certain alterations were made to the building by architect A. F. Shchedrin, and it was then placed at the disposal of the University of St. Petersburg, founded in 1819. Many outstanding men were students here once. In 1891, Lenin sat for his examinations in the Council Hall of the University after completing his extra-mural course of study in law. There is a memorial plaque commemorating this occasion. Prominent Russian scientists worked here for many years—Mendeleyev (whose flat in the University building has been made into a museum), Sechenov, Butlerov, Miklukho-Maklai, Dokuchayev and Popov. Among the writers who received their education at this University we can name Chernyshevsky, Nekrasov, Turgenev and Pisarev.

Its full title now is the Zhdanov Leningrad State University, and it is one of the largest educational institutions in the Soviet Union. In addition to the main building, it occupies several other houses on Vasilyevsky Island, among them the Palace of Peter the Second which, started in 1726, was not completed until several decades later.

The construction of the great city on the Neva offered Russian architects a chance to develop their talent, gain experience and confidence in their skill. In the reign of Peter the Great the training of Russian architects and builders was taken very seriously, and the more gifted young men were sent abroad to study. Among them were Zemtsov, Korobov and Yeropkin, who in 1720–1730 were acclaimed the city's leading architects.

Zemtsov took part in building the Summer Garden and the Palace of Peter the Second, and also designed a number of buildings in the city and its suburbs. The St. Simon's and St. Anna's Church on the corner of Mokhovaya and Belinsky streets, built by him in 1731–1734, has survived. In many ways it resembles the St. Peter's and St. Paul's Cathedral. Like Trezzini, Zemtsov placed the dominating bell tower over the western part

St. Panteleimon's Church

St. Simeon's Church

of the building. The tower is also tiered and topped with a spire. But, as differing from the St. Peter's and St. Paul's Cathedral, the spire does not thrust skyward as impetuously, and all the lines of the church are more flowing and moderate. In the St. Simon's and St. Anna's Church the dominating role of the bell tower is not as pronounced, owing to the size of the cupola over the altar which Zemtsov made much larger than Trezzini's. For all that, the likeness between these two early eighteenth century buildings is obvious.

Not far from the St. Simon's and St. Anna's Church, in Pestel Street, stands the St. Panteleimon's Church built in the seventeen-thirties by Korobov after the brilliant victories won by the Russian Navy at Cape Hangö and Grönhamn. The names and numbers of the units which had fought in these battles are carved on marble memorial panels affixed to the walls of the church.

Both Zemtsov and Korobov worked on the "Commission of St. Petersburg Construction" set up in 1737 to rebuild the Admiralteyskaya Storona (the Admiralty Side) where a considerable part of the buildings were razed to the ground in the great fires of 1736 and 1737. The work of the Commission was organised and directed by P. M. Yeropkin, mentioned earlier. He drew up the plan which outlined the course of the city's further development. At that time, two prospekts—later named the Nevsky and the Voznesensky (now the Mayorov Prospekt)—radiated from the Admiralty, and to these Yeropkin added a third one—Gorokhovaya Street (Dzerzhinsky Street today). These three radiating streets, crossed in an arc by the rivers, canals and streets, actually form the city centre.

The new Hermitage building

W hereas in the first thirty years monumental buildings and structures were mainly erected on the islands off the right bank of the Neva, in the seventeen-thirties and fifties this type of construction was carried on almost exclusively on the Admiralty Side. The most eminent courtiers had their palaces built there, many of which have survived. There is the Sheremetyev Palace (34, Fontanka Embankment), the Anichkov Palace (39, Nevsky Prospekt), the Vorontsov Palace (26, Sadovaya Street) and the Stroganov Palace (17, Nevsky Prospekt).

The Sheremetyev Palace was built in 1750–1755 by two outstanding architects—S. I. Chevakinsky and F. S. Argunov, the latter a serf of Count Sheremetyev. The main façade, which has been preserved except for a few changes, stretches along the embankment behind a fancy cast-iron grille and a small front court. The central part of the façade is decorated with six pilasters, a balcony and an attic, and the right and left parts with pilasters and small pediments. The twin wings at each end of the façade form one whole with the palace. By framing the windows in wide, ornamental platbands with barely any plain space left between them and by lavishly applying decorative moulding, the architects achieved an effect of festivity and joie de vivre.

The former Sheremetyev Palace

The Zhdanov Palace of Young Pioneers (formerly Anichkov Palace)

Anichkov Palace. Red drawing room

The Anichkov Palace on the opposite bank of the Fontanka, not far from the Sheremetyev Palace, was started in 1741. It was reconstructed several times by prominent architects, and took on a different look every time. Zemtsov designed the original palace and grounds on the corner of Nevsky Prospekt and the Fontanka Embankment and started the construction, but he died two years later before he could do more than lay the foundation. V. V. Rastrelli was then commissioned, and he completed the building, using the general plan drawn up by Zemtsov.

Early in the 19th century, Quarenghi was asked to design a building for "His Majesty's Office" in front of the Anichkov Palace on Nevsky Prospekt, and also a colonnade for the drive-in from the Fontanka Embankment.

The palace derived its name from its proximity to the Anichkov Sloboda where a squad of seamen working in construction was billeted under the supervision of an officer whose name was Anichkov. Empress Elizabeth, on whose orders the palace was built, made a present of it to Count Razumovsky. Later, it was bought by the crown and until the Revolution remained the property of the royal family.

Since 1937 it has been the Palace of Young Pioneers, a very popular place with the young Leningraders where they attend various art and hobby circles. The interior was reconstructed by a group of architects, headed by A. I. Gegello.

In the middle of the 18th century St. Petersburg did not yet spread beyond the Fontanka, and the nobles preferred to build their mansions here, away from the noise and bustle of the city, where there was plenty of vacant land and where they felt as comfortable as they would in their sprawling country estates.

And country estates is what many of the palaces built as the time resembled most. The Vorontsov Palace for one, built in 1749–1757 by V. V. Rastrelli, the greatest architect of the period. He came to Russia as a boy of fifteen with his father, a well-known sculptor, whom Peter the Great had invited to work here. Young Rastrelli made a close study of Russian architecture, and his later creations were clearly influenced by the traditions of picturesque 17th century Moscow architecture.

The former Vorontsov Palace   The former Stroganov Palace

The Vorontsov Palace, like most of these country mansions, was set far back from the road in the middle of a park plot with a formal front court-yard leading to the gates of the wrought iron fence. Seen from Sadovaya Street, the façade presents a most striking picture, and it seems all the more impressive for the low service wings placed perpendicularly to it at the sides. The central part of the façade is slightly projecting and is a storey higher than the rest of the building. And the higher the structure, the less weighty it looks. There are groups of columns flanking the front entrance; on the second floor only the end windows are framed in twin columns, with pilasters between the three middle windows; and the top floor has neither columns nor pilasters and all it has for adornment are plain piedroits. There is no wall space at all: the windows, set close together, are surrounded by an intricately designed moulding, and columns, pilasters and piedroits fill in the remaining space. The impression of festive picturesqueness is in-creased by the bright colouring of the palace, whose interior decoration is a match for the exterior.

Contrarily, the Stroganov Palace, built by Rastrelli in 1752–1754, bears no resemblance to a country estate. This is a palace of the urban type. It stands on the corner of Nevsky Prospekt and the Moika Embankment, keeping strictly in line with the other buildings on these two streets. The architect's anxiety not to disturb this line is evident in his treatment of the façades. There is not a single sharply projecting part, and the numerous ornaments merely emphasise the length of the building. In the centre of the Nevsky façade there is an arched gateway through which the coaches drove into the front court. A mask in the shape of a lion's head is inset above the arch which is flanked by double columns supporting a small broken pediment. The platband round the window above the arch is lavishly decorated with stucco moulding and figures of the Atlantes, placed in pro-file. All the other platbands of the main floor are as decorative with a lion's mask at the top and a medallion with a man's profile in haut relief at the bottom. The ones round the windows of the first and third floors are much more modest in size and decoration. This is common to most palace buildings where the second storey (or the first floor, whichever way one wants to call it) was reserved for the "best" rooms.

"Madonna Lita", Leonardo da Vinci (Hermitage
Museum)

Winter Palace. View from the Neva

The two façades of the Stroganov Palace are not identical. The same decorations are used but in different combinations. For instance, the central part of the Moika façade is offset by six semi-columns, uniting the two top storeys, and the corner of the building is rounded off with pilasters.

The interior of the palace was completely done over in the seventeen-nineties by Andrei Voronikhin, a brilliant Russian architect who began life as a serf of Count Stroganov. The exterior remained unchanged.

A striving for ornateness and magnificence, typical for mid-eighteenth century architecture, is apparent in the Sheremetyev, the Vorontsov and the Stroganov palaces, and even more pronounced in the Winter Palace, built by Rastrelli in 1754–1762.

The Winter Palace was to occupy a most important site, and its architecture would, to a large extent, determine the character of the city's centre. There was a palace here already, built in the seventeen-thirties, but it was too small and plain, and so it was decided to erect a new one in its place.

Comparing it with the other palaces built at the beginning of the century, makes the change in artistic tastes immediately obvious. The simplicity and reserve that distinguished the earlier architecture had been completely ousted. Everything had to be ornate, magnificent and sumptuous. And everything had to be done on a different scale: the Winter Palace has 1050 rooms, 117 staircases, 1886 doors and 1945 windows. Its principal cornice is almost two kilometres long. How small Peter the Great's and his courtiers' houses seem in comparison!

What caused this change in tastes, one might ask? As absolute monarchy became stabilised in Russia and as the nobility gained in wealth and power, the craving of the aristocracy for luxury and ostentatious display mounted irrepressibly. The more power a nobleman had at court, the more dazzling he wanted his palace to be. Fabulous sums were spent on the decoration of the reception halls and family rooms, the costliest materials were imported, and the most famous artists were commissioned. In the creations of the great architects, however, the demands of the court circles found an entirely different interpretation. For them the magnificence of the palace buildings was an expression of Russia's greatness and might. Significantly,

Rastrelli wrote that he was building the Winter Palace "solely for the glory of all Russia."

The palace is literally larger than the eye can see. You must first look at it from afar, from the opposite bank of the Neva, then come closer, cross the bridge and the small garden near the Admiralty, and pause in Palace Square to ponder on the new features that were revealed to you as your angle of vision shifted. The green walls make a striking background for the white columns, platbands, cupids, plaster masks, scrolls, and the statues and vases on the roof. There are so many of them, that at first glance you feel it would be futile trying to find some logic in all this amassment. But you need only walk round the palace and look closely at it to realise that there is, in fact, a clear and precise pattern to it.

In shape, the palace is a rectangle with projecting corners and an inner court. All the façades are differently decorated to suit the character of their environment. In the northern side facing the Neva, everything underlines the extension of the building along the embankment. There is but an insignificant projection in the centre of the façade for a three-span entrance with columns. The side risalitos are very wide and lavishly decorated. The spaces between the windows have decorative columns placed one on top of the other, and twin columns in the central parts of the risalitos. The rhythm is thereby accelerated and, when you look down the façade, the row of white, double-deck columns seems infinite.

The southern façade turned to Palace Square is designed differently. When Rastrelli planned the palace he also envisaged the square in front of it with a monument to Peter the Great in the centre and a circular colonnade. The square was built much later, in the 19th century, and not as Rastrelli planned it. The central part of the façade projects in stages and has three risalitos with three ground-floor arches in the middle of the central one, the middle arch also determining the middle of the square.

Rastrelli achieved the effect of fabulous splendour by employing a great variety of artistic means: the numerous and purely decorative columns, placed on top of one another and here and there gathered in clusters, creating a fanciful play of light and shade against the green background, the

Little Hermitage

Hermitage Theatre

elaborate platbands, of a different pattern for every storey; and last but not least, the sculptural figures of knights, nymphs and goddesses, interspersed with vases, set along the length of the cornice, completing, as it were, the vertical lines formed by the double-tiered columns.

One can easily imagine how fabulously magnificent people thought the Winter Palace two hundred years ago when it gleamed with fresh paint and sparkled with thousands of lights every night.

The interior decoration, designed by Rastrelli, was as magnificent but, unlike the exterior which has been preserved almost intact, little of it has survived. The main vestibule and the Jordan Staircase remain as originally built by Rastrelli. This wide marble staircase is a prelude to the dazzling splendour of the palace halls. The spacious flights, the painted plafonds, the statuary and the columns adorning the balustrade, create this mood of exciting, happy anticipation.

On mounting the Jordan Staircase, the visitor of two hundred years ago entered an endless enfilade of halls, rivalling one another in splendour. In 1837, fire destroyed all the interior decoration of these halls, and they were given a different look by architects A. P. Bryullov and V. P. Stasov who supervised the restoration work.

While admiring Rastrelli's amazing wealth of imagination, we must also pay a tribute to the skill of the workmen who accomplished the great architect's design. Using ordinary carpenter's tools, they made all these elaborate carvings and intricate ornaments, and toiling in all weathers, in freezing cold and in sweltering heat, erected this enormous edifice in a very short space of time, relatively speaking.

The speed with which the masons, plasterers, stucco modellers and marble cutters worked was amazing. And restoration work after the fire of 1837 went at an even faster pace, taking fifteen months in all. The recollections of a contemporary give us some idea of the appalling conditions in which these repairs were done. In the coldest winter months when the temperature dropped to 25—30°C below zero, six thousand men worked on the interior decoration of the rooms heated to 30°C for quicker drying. Since they had to go in and out of the building very often, they suffered all the consequences of this sharp change of temperature. The men who

Zimnyaya Kanavka

New Hermitage

New Hermitage. Statues of the Atlantes

painted the top of the walls and the ceilings, where the heat was at its worst, wore caps filled with ice on their heads in order not to faint.

The Winter Palace was the residence of the royal family until the revolution of February 1917. The bourgeois Provisional Government occupied it in the summer and autumn of 1917, and on the historic night of October 25 (November 7) the palace was seized by the insurgent people, led by Lenin.

Today the State Hermitage, the country's largest museum, exhibits its collections in the Winter Palace and in the four adjacent buildings. The oldest of these—the Little Hermitage—was built next to the palace on the Neva embankment in 1764–1767, with the façade designed by Jean Baptiste de la Motte. The most valuable works of art belonging to the royal family were kept there. Catherine II only admitted a narrow circle of courtiers to view the collections of the Hermitage, as it was fittingly called.

In much of its design, the building of the Hermitage is subordinated to the Winter Palace, copying its height and the horizontal sections devised by Rastrelli. But unlike the palace's mood of ornate jubilance, the Hermitage has an air of quiet restraint. The ground floor has an alternating pattern of rustic work and plain wall surface. The slightly projecting centre is decorated with columns supporting a portico, and the rest of the building—with two-storey high pilasters.

The building soon proved too small for the quickly growing collections, and the Second or Old Hermitage, as it was then called, was built by G. Veldten in 1775–1784. It stands in line with the Winter Palace and the Little Hermitage along the Neva embankment. Rastrelli's rhythmic sectional division is again repeated in the design of this building, which is even plainer and quieter than the Little Hermitage.

Some years later, in 1783–1787, G. Quarenghi built the Hermitage Theatre across Zimnyaya Kanavka from the Old Hermitage and connected with it by a roofed passage. The same proportions are used in the theatre building as in the Little and the Old Hermitages. Once again the rusticated ground floor makes the plinth wall, and a row of columns unites the first and second storeys. Statues of Greek poets and dramatists adorn the façade.

Winter Palace. Throne room

"Voltaire" by Houdon

The semi-circular hall which is decorated with Corinthian semi-columns and statues and where the seats, upholstered in red plush, are arranged in rising tiers, is one of the best theatre halls in the city.

When it was first built it answered the name of Hermitage Theatre perfectly, because as a rule there were no more than ten or twelve people in the audience. Occasions when members of the diplomatic corps were invited to attend a performance were very, very rare, and even then the select audience was only a little larger.

The State Hermitage now uses the premises of the theatre for a lecture hall.

The arch, connecting the theatre with the Old Hermitage, goes very well with the gracefully arched bridge across Zimnyaya Kanavka, making one of Leningrad's most charming spots. Looking from Khalturin Street (formerly Millionnaya Street), the river and the opposite bank appear as in a frame in that space between the arch and the bridge. This corner of Leningrad is famous because it was here that one of the dramatic episodes in Chaikovsky's opera *The Queen of Spades* was enacted.

In 1839–1852, yet another building, called the New Hermitage, was added to the existing complex on the Millionnaya Street side. The central part of the main façade is adorned with ten gigantic figures of the Atlantes (carved from grey granite by sculptor A. I. Terebenev) supporting the balcony. The design of the New Hermitage building was drawn up by L. Klentze, but certain amendments were made to it by the commission in charge of construction which had for its members such prominent architects as V. P. Stasov, A. P. Bryullov and N. Y. Yefimov.

The Hermitage museum was opened in 1852, but admission was limited. It was only after the Great October Socialist Revolution that its doors were flung wide before the population and the collected treasures became the property of the people.

There are not many museums in the world whose collections would equal those of the Hermitage in value, variety and artistic worth. The culture and art of nearly all the world is represented here. Celebrated antique sculpture, Russian applied art, paintings by Leonardo da Vinci, Rubens, Raphael, Rembrandt, Velazquez, Vandyke, and many other unique works of art are

"Old Man in Red", Rembrandt

"The Union of Earth and Water", Rubens

"Woman with a Fan", Renoir

displayed in the five big, connected buildings. Many of the staircases, rooms and vestibules in these buildings are works of art in their own right. For instance: the Jordan Staircase, the St. George Hall (or Large Throne Room), the Gallery of the Patriotic War of 1812, the State Emblem room, the main staircase in the New Hermitage, and the Raphael loggias, to name but the finest.

Since the Revolution the collections of the Hermitage have increased more than threefold and continue to grow. Several new departments have been opened, among them the history of Russian culture, and the history of primitive culture. About two and a half million people visit the Hermitage in a year.

By the middle of the eighteenth century, the erection of buildings serving purely practical purposes and badly needed by the growing town was all but suspended and attention was entirely focused on the construction of churches and palaces. The bigger churches and cathedrals built in those years were no less ornate and magnificent than the palaces. For example, the Smolny Nunnery and the Nikolsky (St. Nicholas) Cathedral.

The name Smolny comes from the Smolny Dvor (Tar Yard) situated in the curve of the Neva where, in the reign of Peter the Great, tar needed for shipbuilding was stored and distilled. All the buildings erected here later received the name of Smolny, and the whole of that part of town was called the Smolninsky district.

Rastrelli was commissioned by Empress Elizabeth, the daughter of Peter the Great, to build the nunnery where she intended to retire in her old age. In view of this, he designed it as a palace-nunnery, and construction began in 1748.

The Empress stipulated that her nunnery should be modelled on the five-domed Church of the Assumption in the Moscow Kremlin, with a bell tower similar to that of Ivan the Great. Under Rastrelli's personal supervision a scale model was made of the ensemble, including the bell tower at the entrance to the nunnery which was to be more than 140 metres tall. The model has been preserved, and is on display in the Academy of Arts Museum in Leningrad. Rastrelli died before the finishing work on the other buildings in the ensemble (except the Nunnery itself) was done. This was

Cathedral in the former Smolny Nunnery

completed much later, in the 1830s, by V. P. Stasov who carefully maintained the style and the peculiar features of the original composition.

The former Smolny Nunnery is one of the most interesting monuments of eighteenth-century architecture. The five-domed cathedral, the principal building in the ensemble, is seen from afar for its central dome is 80 metres high. Vividly painted in two colours and lavishly decorated, the cathedral is akin to the palaces designed by Rastrelli, but at the same time it is reminiscent of ancient Russian churches. In olden times, monasteries were also strongholds, and were usually enclosed within fortress walls with watch towers and great, securely locked gateways. Rastrelli also gave his ensemble an enclosed shape, placing the cells in the shape of a cross round the cathedral whose outlines they repeated. But in this case it was just an artistic device, a part of the integral composition. Rastrelli observed a strictly symmetrical pattern, unlike the architects of the ancient monasteries who believed in placing their buildings in a free, asymmetrical manner. He set the cells on either side of the main axis leading from the main gates (where the bell tower was meant to be) to the cathedral. He then built four one-dome churches at the four concave corners of the cells surrounding the cathedral, to emphasise the rhythm of the whole structure. The Smolny cathedral does not have a pronounced main façade, and looks equally well from all sides.

Rastrelli followed traditional Russian five-domed ecclesiastical architecture in just one feature—the predominance of the central dome over the others. But for the rest, he took a novel course. Whereas in ancient churches the domes are usually similar in shape and only differ in size, in the Smolny Cathedral they also differ in shape.

Like the Winter Palace, the Smolny Nunnery has an astonishing abundance of various decorative details: curves, convex and concave surfaces, clusters of decorative columns and pilasters, and elaborate stucco moulding on the platbands.

The old Smolny Nunnery has become even better-looking since the reconstruction of the square, named Rastrelli, in front of it with a small, circular flower garden in the middle.

The Nikolsky (St. Nicholas) Cathedral, built at the intersection of the

The bell tower of St. Nicholas' Cathedral

Kryukov and Yekaterininsky (since renamed Griboyedov) canals in 1753 –1762 by S. I. Chevakinsky, a gifted contemporary of Rastrelli, has a great deal in common with the Smolny Nunnery. With an inventiveness worthy of Rastrelli, Chevakinsky used every variety of ornament to give his cathedral a festive look. There are white columns, gathered in clusters, which stand out well against the pale-blue background and create an effect of light and shade. The large windows have moulded platbands on which cherubs peep out from behind clouds, and the top oval windows are framed in elaborate stucco garlands.

On the bank of the Kryukov canal, at a distance from the cathedral, stands the bell tower also designed by Chevakinsky. Its graceful silhouette seems to dissolve in the sky. Decorative columns soften the dividing line between the three tiers. Proximity to the ornate cathedral enhances the quiet dignity of the modestly decorated tower beautifully reflected in the still waters of the canal.

Monument to Peter I

Towards the end of the seventeen-sixties new tendencies became apparent in the architectural design of public and palace buildings especially.

This was evidenced by the Academy of Arts, built on Vasilyevsky Island, on the banks of the Neva close to Menshikov's Palace in 1764—1788 by A. F. Kokorinov and Jean Baptiste de la Motte. The façade of the Academy, like that of the Winter Palace, stretches along the embankment, but unlike Rastrelli's creation it is devoid of any decorative details and produces an impression of restrained power. The evenly spaced identical pilasters, the end risalitos outlining the corners of the building, and the sharply projected central part—everything is dignified and clear-cut.

The ground floor plays the part of a plinth, as it does in the other major constructions of the seventeen-sixties and seventies, and the two upper storeys are united by columns and pilasters. As different from the country estate type of mansions where a front courtyard always had to be traversed in order to reach the main entrance, the front door of the Acad-

Academy of Arts

emy of Arts building is placed in the middle of the main façade. A four-column portico is raised above the ground floor, with the statues of Hercules and Flora placed between the columns, and the whole of this projecting part of the façade is crowned with a cupola.

The building is rectangular in shape with a circular inner court to ensure good lighting for the classrooms. The interior of the building is efficiently planned and decorated with simple dignity.

The Academy (founded in 1757) trained students in the "three noblest arts"–painting, sculpture and architecture. Among its graduates who brought fame to Russian art were the Ukrainian bard Taras Shevchenko, sculptors F. I. Shubin, M. I. Kozlovsky, and M. M. Antokolsky; architects V. I. Bazhenov, I. Y. Starov and A. D. Zakharov; and painters D. G. Levitsky, K. P. Bryullov, I. Y. Repin, and V. I. Surikov.

The building now houses the Repin Institute of Painting, Sculpture and Architecture.

There is a break in the continuous line of the granite Neva embankment in front of the Academy building where stairs designed by K. A. Thon in 1832–1834 go down to the water. Two sphynxes, brought over from Thebes, the ancient capital of Upper Egypt, are mounted on pedestals flanking the stairs.

There is a small garden next to the Academy of Arts on the bank of the Neva, and in the middle of it stands a tall granite obelisk, designed by V. F. Brenna in honour of the victories scored by Field Marshal Rumyantsev in 1768–1776. Originally, it stood on the Field of Mars, but in the eighteen-twenties it was moved to Vasilyevsky Island and set up in front of the former Cadet Corps where Rumyantsev was educated.

Some of the features that characterise the architecture of the Academy of Arts are also to be found in other public buildings of that period. The architects who designed them did not strive for ornateness and sumptuousness any longer, but they never lost sight of the fact that this was the capital, and that even the purely practical buildings had to fit in with the

One of the two Sphinxes in front of the Academy of Arts

Rumyantsev Obelisk

general appearance of the city centre. Such, for instance, is the Gostiny Dvor (a shopping centre) on Nevsky Prospekt, built in 1761–1785 by de la Motte. This two-storey building faces four streets, and has a perimeter of more than a kilometre. There are numerous shops behind the open double-tier arcade which encircles the whole building. Of interest is the rounded corner on Nevsky and Perinnaya Street which very smoothly links the two long façades. This part of the building has survived in its original form.

A great deal of thought was given to the matter of building a Gostiny Dvor on the principal street of the capital before the project was actually implemented. In the 18th century, a Gostiny Dvor was an inevitable feature of any at all decent town. St. Petersburg had its shopping arcades from the very beginning, but with the passage of years and the increase of trade, their size and location did not satisfy the merchants and the buyers, any longer. It was then decided to build a large Gostiny Dvor, and Rastrelli was commissioned to design it. The building he proposed to erect was as elaborate and sumptuous as all his other creations. His design was found too expensive and the job was given to Jean Baptiste de la Motte instead. This project was much more modest although it was not completely lacking in impressiveness especially in the design of the drive-ins and the façade fronting on Nevsky Prospekt, St. Petersburg's main thoroughfare.

During the Great Patriotic War, bombings and fire did serious damage to the building, but it has now been reconstructed and the numerous small shops have been merged into what is today one of the largest department stores in the city.

There is a certain resemblance in small things between the Gostiny Dvor and the Novaya Gollandia (New Holland) warehouses also built in the seventeen-sixties. New Holland was the name given to a small island, formed by the Moika and the branches of the Admiralty Canal, where ship timber was stored. The low warehouses (built by Chevakinsky) rising taller towards the centre, were connected by a brick arch designed by de la Motte. This seemingly crude arch is impressive in its sternness.

The magic play of colours and the ornateness which distinguished the creations of Rastrelli and his contemporaries were no longer the fashion, as we see from the Academy of Arts, the Gostiny Dvor and the New Holland arch. A tendency towards formal simplicity was also apparent in the palace buildings of the seventeen-sixties and seventies. Of particular interest is the Marble Palace, built in 1768–1785 by Antonio Rinaldi for Count Grigory Orlov. It concludes the row of palatial buildings adjoining the Winter Palace, and architecturally has a great deal in common with them. The façades of the Marble Palace, facing the Neva embankment and Khalturin (formerly Millionnaya) Street, are decorated with laconic simplicity. The ground floor is faced with a brownish granite, and the two main floors are adorned with two-storey Corinthian pilasters alternating in a rhythmical pattern with the windows framed in plain platbands.

The main façade which faces an inner court is closer in style to the seventeen-fifties. There is a huge semi-circular window above the ground-floor entrance, with smaller semi-circular windows to the right and left of it. Four decorative Corinthian columns, placed between these windows, support an imposing attic, adorned with statues and a clock tower. In contrast to the severe façades overlooking the street, there is an abundance of purely decorative effects here, curved lines and ornate details reminiscent of Rastrelli's palaces.

Originally, the two main floors of the palace were faced on the outside and the inside with marble (hence the name) of different colours, matched with exquisite taste. Grey marble was chosen to make a background for the white pilasters, and faintly veined slabs of pastel hues were used to edge the main floor and offset the dark granite facing of the plinth. The marble came from Finland, the Urals, Italy and other places thousands of miles away. The palace, clothed in marble, was considered one of the most impressive buildings in St. Petersburg. Its halls and chambers had

The "New Holland" Arch

Leningrad Branch of the Central Lenin Museum (formerly the Marble Palace). View from Khalturin Street

Leningrad Branch of the Central Lenin Museum (formerly the Marble Palace). Main entrance

"Lenin takes the floor" by Brodsky

floors made from the most valuable kinds of wood of different colours, painted plafonds, and were adorned with the sculptures by F. I. Shubin and M. I. Kozlovsky. But as in the case of most buildings of that period, the interior has been completely altered and only the main staircase has survived.

The Marble Palace is now the Leningrad branch of the Lenin Museum where rare documents relating to the life and revolutionary activity of the great founder of the Communist Party and the Soviet state have been collected.

An old armoured car stands on a pedestal in the centre of the small court in front of the main entrance to the museum. The words: "The Enemy of Capital" are inscribed in dark red letters on the turret. This armoured car is a unique historico-revolutionary monument. Standing on the steel platform of this car, parked in front of Finland Station, Lenin made his famous speech on his return from emigration to Russia on April 3, 1917, which he concluded by calling on the proletariat to fight for a socialist revolution.

As more excellent buildings appeared on the riverside, it became increasingly apparent how badly the view was spoilt by the dirty banks. Facing them with granite and building an embankment was absolutely essential for the general appearance of the city. This job, which was the largest construction project in St. Petersburg, was started in the seventeen-sixties and finished twenty-five years later, in which time more than thirty kilometres of granite embankment were built. The scale on which this project was launched had no precedent in the world.

The splendour of the palaces, public buildings and squares on the left bank of the Neva was enhanced by the four-kilometre long stone wall that had the same quality of sternness and power as the river itself. The physical peculiarities of the Neva delta and the elevation of the banks were taken into good account by the architects. The keynote of the embankment was a stern and solemn dignity. There are no curved lines or fancy ornaments, and the solid line of the wall is broken only by the semi-circular stairs leading down to the water and the small bridges over the Fontanka and the canals. The architects in charge of the project realised very well that in a city crossed by so many waterways this had to be an artistically done job. The Neva embankments are indeed among the city's greatest adornments, and it is not surprising that Pushkin began his inspired hymn to St. Petersburg with the words:

> *I love you, Peter's great creation,*
> *The solemn grace of your design,*
> *The Neva with its flow majestic,*
> *The granite of its stern confines.*

Embankments were also built on the Fontanka, the Moika and the Yekaterininsky (now Griboyedov) canal, and bridges were thrown across all these waterways.

Ah, the bridges of Leningrad! Volumes could be written about them. There are hundreds of them, they are all different and yet alike in something. There are long and short bridges, wide and narrow bridges, stone and wooden bridges, bridges across the broad Neva, the still canals, the serenely flowing Fontanka and the winding Moika. They make an organic part of Leningrad which cannot be pictured without them.

The first bridge over the Neva was built in 1727 to connect the Admiralty and the Vasilyevsky Island. The number of bridges connecting other islands increased steadily with the years. The humped little bridges that seem to be woven into the granite embankments, the tiny Bankovsky Bridge with its gilded griphons, and the bridges across the Fontanka with their stone turrets and hanging chains, lend infinite charm to their environments. The oldest of the existing bridges over the Neva is hardly a hundred years old. Construction began in the middle of the last century. The first to appear was the Nikolayevsky (now the Lt. Schmidt) Bridge, then the Liteiny, much

Palace Bridge at night   Lomonosov Bridge over the Fontanka later—at the beginning of this century—came the Troitsky (now Kirovsky), later still—the Okhtinsky, the Dvortsovy and the Circuit Railway bridges, the Volodarsky bridge, and finally the Alexander Nevsky bridge. Differing in construction and appearance, these bridges complement the general panorama of the embankments with their cast-iron openwork railings, massive stone abutments, and the silhouettes of their arched spans.

The work of building bridges and facing the river banks with granite is still going on. Alterations have been made to the Arsenalnaya and Pirogov-skaya embankments in Vyborgskaya Storona; three new bridges have been built across the Bolshaya Nevka and Malaya Nevka—the Ushakovsky, the Kamenno-Ostrovsky and the Svoboda, and two across the Malaya Neva—the Stroitelei Bridge (1960) and the Tuchkov Bridge (1965).

Construction of the Alexander Nevsky bridge, the longest in Leningrad, was completed in November 1965. It connects Nevsky Prospekt with Malaya Okhta, one of the most important new residential districts.

Building the granite embankments was not the only city development project implemented in the seventeen-sixties and eighties. New houses, roads and squares were built in the centre of St. Petersburg. The contrast between its palatial splendour and the appalling poverty of the outskirts, where the greater part of the population lived in hovels, became more and more glaring.

The plan of the city's development, proposed by Yeropkin, was continued by A. V. Kvasov who drew up a plan of reconstructing the Admiralty Storona. Kvasov was the leading architect of the "St. Petersburg and Moscow Stone-Building Commission" established in 1762 in place of the old urban construction offices.

The Commission was confronted by challenging problems. The development of industry and trade was forcing the city's growth, and chaotic construction was going on apace in what was until then regarded as outside the city limits. The Commission's immediate task was to establish law and order in St. Petersburg's building. However, the ambitious plans drawn up

Bank Bridge

Lion Bridge

Kamenno-ostrovsky Bridge

Kirov Bridge

by Kvasov for the Commission were only realised in small part. The rest was either dropped altogether or only implemented at a much later period.

The granite embankments lent a new quality to the ensembles and squares on the banks of the Neva. One of these squares, next to the Admiralty wharf, is called the Decembrists' Square (originally it was called Petrovskaya and then Senatskaya). Adorning this square is the famous equestrian monument to Peter the Great—the "Bronze Horseman" celebrated by Pushkin—one of the most perfect creations in the monumental sculpture of the world.

The monument was unveiled on August 7, 1782. As guns fired a salute, the scaffolding, painted to look like rough stone and screening the monument, collapsed and the bronze figure of Peter the Great on the peak of a granite rock came into view before the thousands of people gathered in the square.

The sculptor, Etienne Maurice Falconet, portrayed Peter as the statesman and great reformer. He showed Peter at a moment of dramatic tension, reining in his rearing horse, with a snake writhing at its feet, on the edge of a precipice. Although allegory was commonly used by the sculptors of that period, there is hardly any in this monument, except for the rock which symbolises the obstacles surmounted by Peter, and the snake—a symbol of envy, narrow-mindedness and spite, that interfered with Peter and his reforms. Instead of royal robes, the laurel-crowned rider wears a loose cape, and in place of a saddle he has the skin of an animal, true to ancient custom. He is a man, and not an effigy of a ruler, a monarch. This ascetic simplicity, so unusual for eighteenth century sculpture, has been explained by Falconet himself as follows: "My monument will be simple .... I want to make a statue of a hero, and I am not going to portray him as a great military commander and conqueror, although he was both, of course. The personality of the creator, the law-maker, is much higher ...."

The large square seemed even larger in the 18th century when there were no buildings nearby. Falconet used the peculiar features of the site to place the monument to the best advantage where it would be as impressive from whatever point it was viewed. The whole composition conveys impetuous movement forward and upward, but different features are revealed from different angles. Looking from the Senate, from the western edge of the square, one is most impressed by the impetuosity of the rearing horse. From the opposite side, one is struck first of all by the imperiously confident gesture of Peter's right arm, outstretched towards the Neva. Standing in front of the monument, one fancies that the horse is about to leap down and trample everything in its path.

The granite rock which makes the pedestal has the following words inscribed in Russian on one side: "To Peter I From Catherine II. 1782," and in Latin on the other: "Petro Primo—Catherina Secunda MDCCLXXXII."

The "Bronze Horseman" was Falconet's masterpiece, unequalled by anything he ever created before or afterwards.

He arrived in St. Petersburg in 1766 for the express purpose of building a monument to Peter. Realising full well the importance of the work he was entrusted with, Falconet went about it with unhurried meticulousness. From the recollections of his contemporaries we know some details of how he tackled the job. On his instructions, a platform, shaped somewhat like the pedestal we see today, was erected in front of his apartment, not far from the site of the monument. Riders charged up this platform at full gallop and reined in their horses again and again, while Falconet stood watching them and making sketches. His patient toil was crowned with complete success: the impulse of the galloping horse in fusion with the rider has been rendered dynamically.

Falconet's young pupil Marie-Anne Collot assisted him, and it was she who moulded the head of the rider. The likeness to Peter is remarkable, and the head is one of the best features of the monument. The stern expression on Peter's strong, energetic face and the way he sits his horse harmonise so perfectly with the whole figure of the rider that one imagines it is all the work of one sculptor.

Decembrists' Square

The heavy, six-metre-tall group, Falconet felt, should have three points of support. The third point is made by the writhing snake which is connected with the horse's tail. Sculptor Fyodor Gordeyev, who designed the snake, executed Falconet's scheme so artfully that the snake is accepted as an organic part of the composition.

Part of the credit for the Bronze Horseman goes to Khailov, a caster of outstanding skill, who besides executing the highly intricate casting job with excellence also displayed great courage and quickness in rescuing the figure when a fire broke out in the workshop. Owing to faults in the mould, the liquid metal spilled over on to the floor, and all the objects made of wood caught fire at once. Everyone there was paralysed with shock and fright. Khailov alone did not lose his presence of mind and, undaunted by the danger to his life and getting badly burnt, put out the fire. Falconet said of Khailov: "We owe the success of the casting to his courage."

There is also a story to the pedestal. This huge granite rock, called a "thunder-stone," weighing about fifteen hundred tons, was found by Semyon Vishnyakov, a peasant, near Lakhta, a village in the Karelian Isthmus, fifteen kilometres away from the centre of St. Petersburg. And this is how it was delivered to the site: the rock was first levered on to a log platform running on copper balls on specially grooved rails, and dragged to the shore of the Gulf of Finland, and then loaded on a specially constructed barge and hauled to Senate Square. A special medal was made in memory of this heroic endeavour. Transporting the rock took about two years, in the course of which the granite was shaped according to Falconet's design. The upward lines of the pedestal make one think of a rising surf.

Standing in admiration before the monument one involuntarily remembers Pushkin's immortal lines:

> *How dread his image in the night!*
> *Upon his brow what thoughts of might!*

The strength with which he is endowed!
How mettlesome his horse, how proud!
Oh, fiery steed, where are you bound,
And where your hoofs you will bring down?
Ah, mighty lord of destiny!
Was it not thus, with iron hand
That at disaster's very brink
You reared on high the Russian land?

In the past this place was called the Senatskaya (Senate) Square because the small building of the Senate stood on its western edge, on the corner of the embankment. New and much more imposing buildings of the Senate and the Synod were erected in its place in 1829–1834 when construction in the city's centre was already nearing completion, and are still in perfect condition. They were the last major creation of Carlo Rossi, an architect of outstanding talent. The two independent buildings, decorated with loggias and numerous marble figures, are connected by a triumphal arch built over Galernaya (now Krasnaya) Street. Rossi skilfully followed the proportions and sectional divisions of the side façade of the Admiralty, finished a little earlier and facing the opposite side of the square.

Occupied with other projects, Rossi was unable to supervise this construction personally, and another architect (A. J. Staubert) had to be appointed to finish the job. The project suffered even more damage from the interference of Nicholas I and the holy fathers from the Synod who demanded that many of the decorations should be changed. The architect's original design was therefore violated, and as a result the parts of the two buildings adjoining the arch were overloaded with ornaments. On the whole, however, the Senate and the Synod completed the ensemble of the square quite happily. Nowadays, the two buildings house the Central State Historical Archives.

Senatskaya Square was renamed Decembrists' Square in honour of those

The former Senate Building

Arch connecting the former Senate and Synod

Russian revolutionaries of the nobility who were the first to attempt an armed uprising against the autocracy. The uprising took place on December 14, 1825, (hence the name Decembrists) during the interregnum after the death of Alexander I. Early that morning, several regiments led by officers who belonged to secret revolutionary societies entered the square. The insurgents refused to take the oath to the new tsar Nicholas I. Standing in square formation round the monument to Peter the Great, they repelled several attacks of the government troops, waiting for orders to take action themselves. The orders, however, were not forthcoming. Prince Trubetskoi, the appointed "dictator" of the Decembrists, simply stayed away, while the other leaders of the rebellion showed hesitancy. The sympathies of the population, it must be said, lay with the insurgents. Stones and logs of wood were hurled at the government troops from St. Isaac's Cathedral which was then under construction, and rebellious shouts against the new tsar were heard. It was obvious that the "lower" sections of the population were prepared to join the insurgents at a word. But the leaders of the Decembrists did not make use of this opportunity, and their vacillation allowed the government troops to surround the square and bring in their artillery, which decided the outcome of the uprising.

Ruthless reprisals followed the suppression of the uprising. Five of the Decembrists' leaders were hanged on the crownwork outside the Peter and Paul Fortress, about 120 insurgents were sentenced to hard labour, and many of the soldiers were made to run the gauntlet. The defeat of the uprising, however, could not prevent the spread of freedom-loving ideas. The example of the Decembrists inspired the finest members of Russian society to wage an energetic and dedicated struggle against tsarism.

Many of Leningrad's streets and squares are named after the participants in this first armed uprising against the autocracy, people whom Lenin called the first generation of Russian revolutionaries.

Smolny

As the town expanded, the nobles built their estates further and further away from its palatial centre. In the seventeen-fifties the region of the Fontanka was the most favoured locality, and by the seventeen-eighties there was not a single vacant plot left. And so they had to look further afield for a suitable site, to beyond the Fontanka and to places further south and south-west which were either vacant or built up with structures of no importance.

Thus, the Taurida Palace for Prince Potyomkin was built at a considerable distance from the centre, near the bend of the Neva. I. Y. Starov, a leading architect of the time, designed the palace which took from 1783 to 1789 to build. In character it is like a great country estate, and the house itself has survived with hardly any alterations.

We find that here the ornateness of Rastrelli's palaces has been completely ousted and superseded by a simple, quiet dignity. The main building, placed at the back of a formal front court, has two wings, built at right angles to it and connected with it by single-storey passages. The court in front of the main façade opens on to the Neva.

Unlike Rastrelli, Starov used no ornaments whatsoever to break the monotony of the walls. On the contrary, he rather emphasised it by leaving the surface between the rectangular windows, without platbands, completely plain and only offsetting the centre of the main façade and the ends of the wings with porticoes. The columns play a constructive and not merely a decorative role. There are no sculptured ornaments, no pilasters, no stucco moulding on the platbands, no decorations at all. Starov achieves his artistic effect by well-balanced proportions and general harmony. The poet Derzhavin wrote of this palace that: "There is no display of carving, gilding or any other costly ornaments. It is distinguished by ancient elegant taste: it is plain but majestic."

The main building makes the centre of this very clear-cut, logical and strictly symmetrical composition. The architect stresses the length of the façade by uniting the wings and the connecting passages with a common cornice. Besides the Doric portico which looks imposing against the plain and not very tall walls, there is a beautifully shaped wide, low cupola over the central part of the façade. The palace building was ingeniously integrated into the landscape of the Neva's low banks, and we can judge from the canvases of 18th century painters how majestic it looked from the opposite side of the river—from Vyborgskaya Storona. This view is no more because a water-tower and other utility buildings were erected in the space between the main façade and the Neva in late 19th century, which naturally ruined the ensemble as conceived by Starov.

The rear, garden façade of the Taurida Palace is light and graceful. The windows are tall and without platbands, and the narrow spaces between are decorated with Doric pilasters.

Originally, the interior of the palace was the exact opposite of the exterior. While the façades were emphatically simple and severe, the halls were as emphatically resplendent. From the vestibule one entered a won-

Taurida Palace   Taurida Palace. Main Hall

Taurida Palace. View from the garden

derful octagonal hall adorned with murals and moulded ornaments which Derzhavin called "an oval chamber similar to the Athenian Odeum." Behind this hall there was the main hall stretching across the central part of the building and adorned with a double row of Ionic columns. This colonnade, which had no equal in 18th century architecture, evoked unanimous admiration. From the main hall one entered the Winter Garden stocked with a great variety of decorative plants. The huge windows faced the park with its picturesque ponds, and the trees painted in the spaces between the windows created an illusion of this indoor garden being part of the real one outside.

In the centre of the Winter Garden there was a rotunda comprised of eight columns, and under its cupola stood a statue of Catherine II by F. I. Shubin.

Little remained of all this splendour when Paul I, succeeding his mother Catherine II, ascended the throne. Remembering Potyomkin's festivities with abhorrence, he let the Mounted Guards regiment use the palace for barracks, and ordered stables to be built in the finest hall of all. The marble fire-places, parquet floors, sculptured ornaments and furnishings were moved to the tsar's residence, and many of the rooms were rebuilt to suit their new purpose. Within a few years the palace was disfigured so badly that there could be no hope of ever restoring it completely. True, upon ascending the throne, Alexander I did order the palace to be restored to its original state, but this could not be done. Architect Luigi Rusca, who was in charge of the work, had the floor in the main hall raised by about 60 centimetres, which distorted the proportions of the colonnade; he also did away with the rotunda, and made other changes. Some time later, F. Scotti was commissioned to do the murals which have been preserved to this day. After that, the interior of the palace was rebuilt again and again. At the beginning of this century it was reconstructed for the State Duma, and the Winter Garden was converted into a hall where the Duma held its sessions.

The Taurida Palace became widely known in 1917. After the overthrow of the autocracy, it was here that the Petrograd Soviet of Workers' and Soldiers' Deputies began its work. It was here that on April 4, 1917, the day after his return to Russia, Lenin delivered his April Theses in which the Party's policy of developing the bourgeois-democratic revolution into the socialist revolution were defined. Lenin spoke here after the Great October Revolution as well: in 1918 he delivered his report to the Third All-Russia Congress of Soviets and directed the work of the Seventh Party Congress; and on July 19, 1920, on the day of his last visit to Petrograd, he spoke at the opening of the Second Congress of the Comintern.

Today the palace is used for Party and Komsomol conferences, sessions of Soviets, international and all-Union congresses, meetings of front-ranking workers in industry or agriculture, and conferences of scientists and cultural workers. Part of the premises are occupied by the Leningrad Higher Party School.

Since 1917, the interior of the palace underwent several reconstructions, and many of the halls have been given back their original appearance.

The garden behind the palace which is one of the largest and shadiest in Leningrad has been made into a recreation park for children.

The palace was widely imitated in Russian architecture, and for decades "mansions with columns" modelled on it were erected in country estates, whether big or small ones.

Features of classicism, the style which became the predominant one in late eighteenth century architecture, are very distinct in the Taurida Palace. This style took shape gradually. It can be easily traced from the example of the buildings already described how, beginning from the seventeen-sixties, architects gradually renounced the artistic principles prevailing at the middle of the century. As seen from the Taurida Palace, the distinguishing features of classicism were simplicity, compositional clarity, perfection of proportions, logic in the general pattern, severity in the choice of decorations, and competent utilisation of the antique architectural orders.

116

The General Post Office   The Academy of Sciences

The former Currency Bank

Monument to Quarenghi in front of the Currency
Bank

I. Y. Starov was a leading exponent of classicism in Russian architecture. This is further proved by another creation of his—the Troitsky (Trinity) Cathedral at the Alexander Nevsky Lavra.

Peter the Great ordered a *lavra* (a monastery of the highest order) to be built where the Chyornaya River falls into the Neva, believed to be the spot where the Russian armies led by Alexander Nevsky scored their historic victory over the Teutonic Knights. Although the order was given in 1710, the cathedral, which was planned as a mausoleum for Alexander Nevsky, was only built in 1776–1790. In the meantime, the *lavra* grounds were built up round the future cathedral which was to be the pivot of the ensemble for the next 150 years.

Starov designed a classically severe building, vastly different in style from the ornate cathedrals built by Rastrelli and Chevakinsky. As in the Taurida Palace, the exceptionally resplendent interior makes a glaring contrast to the sternly dignified exterior.

A large dome crowns the central part of the building, and two bell towers rise on its western side. For clarity of composition, for the perfect balance of its different parts, and for sheer beauty of silhouette, this cathedral is one of the most interesting examples of late eighteenth century architecture.

Simultaneously with the Troitsky Cathedral, Starov built the chapel over the gate of the Alexander Nevsky Lavra which is the terminal of Nevsky Prospekt.

The *lavra*'s cemetery was opened early in the 18th century, and many prominent military commanders, scientists, poets, composers, artists, architects and actors are buried here. There are two necropolises, and in the one reserved for people in culture and the arts are the graves of Lomonosov, Voronikhin, Zakharov, Rossi, Chaikovsky, Borodin, Stasov, Rimsky-Korsakov, Dostoyevsky, Vera Komissarzhevskaya and many others. Many of the tomb-stones were designed by famous sculptors.

In one of the churches there is a plain marble slab with the inscription:

The former Cavalry Guards manège

"Here Lies Suvorov," marking the last resting place of the great Russian field marshal.

A museum of urban sculpture now occupies one of the church buildings in the *lavra*.

Large-scale construction went on in the centre of St. Petersburg until the end of the 18th century. As the city gained in importance, its economic connections developed, and the population increased. More public buildings were needed–shops, warehouses, hospitals, schools, theatres, libraries, etc.

A large building for the Public Library was erected on the corner of Nevsky Prospekt and Sadovaya Street by architect Y. T. Sokolov; the Naval Academy was built on Vasilyevsky Island with its long and severely plain façade stretching along the Neva embankment (architect F. I. Volkov); and the Post Office (designed by N. A. Lvov) appeared in the vicinity of Senatskaya Square.

The Academy of Sciences, situated between the Kunstkammer and the Twelve Collegia on Vasilyevsky Island, was built in 1783–1789 by Quarenghi. A native of northern Italy, Quarenghi came to Russia in 1779, and it was here that his talent really blossomed. The Academy building was one of his first big assignments.

Its severe laconism is impressive even though the neighbouring early eighteenth century buildings are more dignified than ornate. The powerful, perhaps too heavy, eight-column portico in the centre of the facade dominates the whole neighbourhood. The façade is kept in line with the other buildings, but the front steps are brought forward and take up part of the pavement. Features typical to Russian classicism, such as calm dignity, well-balanced composition and symmetry, are very much in evidence here.

The Academy was transferred to Moscow in 1934, but its Leningrad branches and institutions continue to be housed in this building.

Another large public building erected in the seventeen-eighties is the

Smolny

Currency Bank in Sadovaya Street, not far from Nevsky Prospekt. It was also designed by Quarenghi, and although its façade has a great deal in common with that of the Academy, in composition the two buildings are quite different. The Bank is set far back from the street, behind a front court which one enters through a gate in a cast-iron grille. This three-storey building is not very large, but it looks tall and stately in comparison to the squat, heavy store-houses surrounding it in a semi-circle. A six-column Corinthian portico adorns the central part of the main façade above the rustic ground-floor arcade. The pediment is ornamented with statuary. While emphasising the central part, Quarenghi left the rest of the façade quite plain, except for the rustic facing of the ground floor and the modest platbands round the second-storey windows. Still, the contrast with the surrounding store-houses is evident, and is very much to the advantage of the main building.

Quarenghi's name occurs again and again when we speak of the public buildings erected in St. Petersburg at the turn of the 18th and 19th centuries. Besides the Hermitage Theatre, the Academy of Sciences, the Bank in Sadovaya Street, and several palaces, Quarenghi also designed the Yekaterininsky Institute on the bank of the Fontanka (it now houses a branch of the Saltykov-Shchedrin Public Library), the Cavalry Guards Manège on Konnogvardeisky Boulevard (renamed Bulvar Profsouzov), and the hospital on Liteiny Prospekt (the Kuibyshev Hospital), to name but the major buildings.

The Smolny Institute deserves to be dwelt upon in greater detail. It was built in 1806–1808 next to the Smolny Nunnery designed by Rastrelli, for an aristocratic girls' boarding-school. Quarenghi intentionally placed it far back from the street behind a large open court to allow a view of the whole façade with an eight-column portico in the centre, which looks quite severe in comparison to Rastrelli's ornate buildings.

The rather long façade does not seem monotonous thanks to its fine proportions and the skilfully accentuated central part. As in Quarenghi's

Hall in Smolny

"Lenin in Smolny", Brodsky

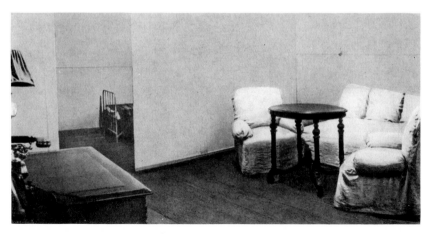

The room in Smolny where Lenin lived and worked

Propilaea at the entrance to Smolny

other buildings, the rooms are spacious and very simply decorated with the exception of the assembly hall in the south wing, adorned with a stately colonnade.

There was a large garden sloping down to the Neva at the back of the main building, and a formal court in front.

The Petrograd Soviet of Workers' and Soldiers' Deputies moved into Smolny on August 4 (17 New Style) of 1917. During the preparations for the armed uprising this was the military headquarters from where the revolutionary struggle of the masses was directed. It was the centre of operations in those historic October days. Lenin lived on the Vyborg Side in hiding from the persecutions of the Provisional Government, and his instructions were brought to Smolny by messengers. On the night of October 24 (November 6) detachments of workers, soldiers and sailors, numbering many thousands, and coming from different parts of the city, converged on the square in front of Smolny. Armed sentries at the front door checked their passes and the stream of people poured into the building. Armoured cars came driving up, more infantry and mounted units arrived. Fires burnt in front of the building all night long, the men sang revolutionary songs and talked. From Smolny the Revolutionary Military Committee despatched the different units to seize such strategic points as the railway stations, bridges, the telegraph office, the telephone exchange, etc.

Lenin arrived at Smolny late that night to assume direction of the operations. Early next morning, October 25, when the town was practically in the hands of the insurgent people, he wrote his appeal "To the Citizens of Russia" in which he announced the overthrow of the Provisional Government and the transference of state power to the Revolutionary Military Committee–a body of the Petrograd Soviet of Workers' and Soldiers' Deputies. It was from Smolny that Lenin proclaimed that day: "The workers' and peasants' revolution, about the necessity of which the Bolsheviks have always spoken, has been accomplished!"

On the evening of October 25 (November 7) while fighting for the Winter Palace was still going on, the Second All-Russia Congress of Soviets opened in Smolny. The world's first government of workers and peasants was formed–the Council of People's Commissars, headed by Lenin,–and the Soviet power's first decrees on peace and land were adopted.

Smolny remained the seat of the Soviet Government until March 1918. In those months (from November to March) Lenin lived in a modest first floor room in the northern wing. The furniture consisting of such bare essentials as beds, a table and chairs, has been preserved. The room has been a museum since 1927, and countless people have come to see it.

Since March 1918, when the Government moved to Moscow, Smolny has been used for offices by the Party and Soviet bodies of Leningrad city and Leningrad region.

In 1923–1925, the space in front of the building was made into a large formal garden, complete with fountains and flower beds, and fenced in from the street with a not very tall, semi-circular grille, elegantly severe in design. Busts of Karl Marx and Frederick Engels, made in the early nineteenth-thirties by sculptor S. A. Yevseyev, have been set up in this garden. Architects V. A. Shchuko and V. G. Gelfreikh built the propylaea, starting from which an avenue, lined with lime trees, goes to the main entrance. The words: "The First Soviet of Proletarian Dictatorship" and "Workers of All Countries, Unite!" are inscribed on the propylaea.

A monument to Lenin (sculptor V. V. Kozlov) was unveiled on the tenth anniversary of Soviet power. The figure is mounted on a round, granite pedestal in front of the main entrance. The leader has his right arm outstretched in an energetic gesture as if calling the people on, to the victory of communism. Lenin's revolutionary ardour, vigorous energy, and inspired faith in a radiant future, have been conveyed by the sculptor by simple, laconic means. Lenin's words: "Long Live the Dictatorship of the Proletariat!" are inscribed on the pedestal.

The once neglected grounds have been converted into one of the finest squares in Leningrad–Proletarian Dictatorship Square. The building itself, the propylaea, the flower garden, and the monuments, form a complete ensemble.

Arch of the General Staff building

Many of the wonderful buildings, monuments, bridges and parks were built in the eighteenth century, but as the city expanded and gained in importance as the capital of a mighty power, it became increasingly obvious that it needed a better-defined formal centre. To accomplish this, the separate buildings had to be united into a system, which was devised and achieved in the first thirty years of the 19th century by A. D. Zakharov, A. N. Voronikhin, Thomas de Thomon, Carlo Rossi and V. P. Stasov.

That period was marked by a striving to build ensembles, rather than single buildings. Elements of ensemble construction are already in evidence in the design of the Engineers' Castle and the adjacent territory. Construction of this castle, for Paul I, was begun in 1797 and completed in 1800. It was built on the site of Elizabeth's old wooden palace, to the south of the Summer Garden, and was originally called Mikhailovsky Castle, in honour of Archangel Michael whom Paul revered as his patron saint. Later, in the eighteen-twenties, it was renamed Engineers' Castle.

The castle holds a place of importance in the architectural ensemble of

Engineers' Castle. Southern façade   Engineers' Castle. Northern façade the city's centre. It is one of the few surviving creations of the brilliant Russian architect V. I. Bazhenov, and his last major work. The actual building was done by Brenna, who changed the original design somewhat, especially in the arrangement of the rooms and the interior decoration. Obviously, he also had a hand in overburdening the façades with architectural details. For all that, Bazhenov's genius is apparent in the general design of the building, in the composition of the façades, and in the way it has been integrated into its surroundings.

The square building has an octagonal yard in the middle. All the four façades are designed differently to suit the view opening before them. The central one, facing the Connetable Square where military parades and reviews were usually held, is impressive in its sinister grandeur. The huge portico raised above a high ground floor, the heavy pediment, and the tall, severe obelisks standing like grim sentries on either side of the gates, give the castle a look of formidable impenetrability. The northern façade overlooking the Summer Garden is entirely different in mood. It is much simpler. At first glance one is surprised by the smallness of the colonnade placed at the top of the wide front staircase, but then one begins to see how well it harmonises with the statuary adorning the Summer Garden and the view of the park before it. The façade of the western wing where the Church of Archangel Michael was housed, has a semi-curcular projection and is crowned with a golden spire. And the opposite, eastern façade has a corresponding projection formed by an oval hall.

Paul I was a morbidly suspicious man, who always feared for his life and never felt secure in the Winter Palace, and so he ordered Bazhenov to build this private residence for him in the style of a medieval castle with a moat and drawbridges, behind which he might feel safe.

While following the Emperor's instructions to the letter, Bazhenov nevertheless managed to create the beginnings of a large, splendid ensemble. Before the main drive-in, on the other side of Connetable Square, he placed identical pavilions, decorating the ground floor with a portico and twin columns, and the two upper floors with a somewhat larger colonnade. These twin pavilions frame the approach to the main façade, further enhancing the castle's air of gloomy solemnity.

Engineers' Castle. Portico of the southern façade

An equestrian statue of Peter the Great, made in the seventeen-forties by K. B. Rastrelli, was erected in Connetable Square in front of the castle gates in 1800. Rastrelli who knew Peter personally took a different approach from Falconet. He portrayed Peter as the emperor, as the stern army leader, and lent the whole of the monument an air of ponderous solemnity. As different from the Bronze Horseman, Rastrelli's laurelled Peter wears the toga of a Roman emperor and sits his stalking horse with majestic calm. His face, which bears a portrait likeness, is formidable in its wrathful strength. Earlier, Rastrelli made an exceptionally expressive bust of Peter.

The pedestal is decorated with embossed pictures of "The Battle at Poltava" (by sculptor I. I. Terebenev) and "The Battle Off Cape Hangö" (by sculptor V. I. Demut-Malinovsky), and bears an inscription made by order of Paul I which says: "From great-grandson to great-grand-father" and the date 1800.

Paul could not wait for his castle to be finished, and he gave the first ball in his new residence before the plaster on the walls had dried which, contemporaries recalled, exuded a horrible vapour. The thick walls and deep moats should have given him the security he craved, but on the forty-first night of his residence there he was strangled in his bed by his own associates. After that, the castle remained unoccupied for a long time. In the eighteen-twenties a school for military engineers (hence the name Engineers' Castle) was opened there.

Later, the grounds in front of the castle were put to an entirely different use, and the beginnings of the ensemble founded by Bazhenov were developed by architects of the next generation, in particular by Carlo Rossi and V. P. Stasov.

The moats were filled in, and in place of the Connetable Square a Maple Avenue was laid connecting the Engineers' Castle with Manezhnaya (Manège) Square. Sadovaya and Inzhenernaya Streets, stretching from the south and west respectively, drew the Castle into the architectural pattern of that neighbourhood. In later years, the ensemble was spoilt by the appearance of various unplanned buildings.

After the Great Patriotic War, architects Y. I. Katonin and V. D. Kirkhoglani reconstructed the Maple Avenue, removing the structures cluttering it, and now it runs to the former Mikhailovsky Manège (now the Winter Stadium) and the former stables with their identical façades, all of which is once again perceived as an integral architectural ensemble.

In the eighteen-thirties construction was most vigorous on the banks of the Neva, and one of the first large new ensembles to appear there was the complex on the Strelka of Vasilyevsky Island. This is the name of the eastern spit of the island where the river forms two arms—the Bolshaya Neva and the Malaya Neva. The port of St. Petersburg, transferred from Gorodskoy Island in the seventeen-thirties, remained here until 1837, for more than a hundred years. For a long time the streets adjoining the port were the liveliest in St. Petersburg: ships flying different flags were berthed

ПРАДѢДУ

ПРАВНУКЪ

1800

Monument to Peter I in front of Engineers'
Castle

at the wharves, goods were loaded and unloaded, there was a perpetual bustle and the hubbub of voices speaking in different languages.

The port is the pride of any maritime town, and it is understandable, therefore, that building up the Strelka was a great challenge to the architects of St. Petersburg, the more so because of its responsible position in the city's general panorama. A large building here would be seen from a long distance away and, what was more, it had to architecturally organise the vast territory and harmonise with the low Neva banks, the Peter and Paul Fortress, and the Hermitage ensemble across the way. Even an architect as gifted as Quarenghi was unable to find a very happy solution to this problem. He placed the Exchange—the central building of the complex—at an angle to the axis of the spit without building an embankment to offset its position. As a result, it got lost among the neighbouring buildings, and naturally failed to serve its purpose as the architectural pivot.

Quarenghi's failure was so obvious that the building, ready to be roofed, was dismantled and the project was entrusted to Thomas de Thomon.

Thomas de Thomon who was educated in France and Italy and was an ardent admirer of antique architecture, came to Russia in 1799 and remained until his death fourteen years later. He belonged to that galaxy of foreign artists who made Russia their second home. Thomas de Thomon submitted his first design to the Academy of Arts in 1801, but in view of its many imperfections approval was withheld. In the course of the next four years, he changed his design six times. The competent criticism of the Academy members helped him to correct the imperfections and successfully accomplish the work. The chief expert was A. D. Zakharov, and his role in achieving the Strelka ensemble can hardly be overestimated. He was the most active and authoritative member of the commission of experts, and Thomas de Thomon altered many details in his design acting on his instructions.

The ceremony of laying the foundation stone of the Exchange was held on June 23, 1805. In the main, the building was finished in 1810, but the Exchange was not opened until June 15, 1816, and Thomas de Thomon did not live to see the day.

To gain a general impression of the complex it is best to look at it from Kirov Bridge, and then the central role played by the Exchange becomes self-evident.

Thomas de Thomon placed the Exchange precisely along the axis of the Strelka and artificially extended the spit for more than 120 metres from the natural shoreline, building on it a semi-circular granite embankment. This serves as a granite foundation for the Exchange placed, besides, on a terrace with broad staircases and ramps on two sides. The building is surrounded and almost hidden from view by forty-four massive Doric columns which support a heavy entablature, above which comes the top part of the building and the high-pitched roof. There are two large semi-circular windows above the entablature in the façades turned to the Strelka and the Twelve Collegia, and these windows make an effective background for the two sculptural groups: the figure of Neptune in a chariot drawn by sea horses with the rivers Neva and Volkhov symbolically flowing around him (on the Strelka side), and the figure of a young woman symbolising the Neva wearing a crown on her head, and standing with Mercury, the patron of trade, surrounded by two rivers. The geometrically precise proportions of the Exchange make a splendid contrast to the soaring spire of St. Peter's and St. Paul's Cathedral and the ornateness of the Winter Palace. The white columns of the Exchange are placed against a greyish-green background, the colour of river water, and this mellow colour combination goes well with the bright green-and-white of the Winter Palace and the sober grey of the fortress walls.

The original interior of the Exchange was a match to its exterior. The vast hall, taking up almost the whole building, where merchants arriving in St. Petersburg made their deals, was astonishing in its magnificence. Large sculptural groups of Mercury and Time were installed in the niches formed by the vaulted ceiling, and statues, allegorically representing Justice, Abundance, Trade and Seafaring (which until then had stood on the brick stoves in the main hall) were later placed beside them. These statues, the vaulted ceiling, the two-column porticoes framing the doors and the plain wall cornices, added to the impression of monumental solemnity.

Engineers' Castle. The foyer

Maple avenue

From the accounts of contemporaries it appears that at the time none of the world's ports had an Exchange like the one in St. Petersburg.

The building has been handed over to the Central Naval Museum whose collections illustrate the glorious history of the Russian and Soviet Navy.

All the structures on the Strelka are artistically linked with the Exchange. Its central position is stressed by the two Rostral Columns (30 metres high) in front of it. They were designed by Thomas de Thomon and erected at the same time as the Exchange. They are a reminder of the ancient tradition to celebrate naval victories by erecting triumphal columns adorned with the beaks or rostra of defeated enemy galleys. Seen close to, these brick columns, painted a drab brown, appear rather crude. The five-metre tall allegorical figures at the foot representing four Russian rivers—the Volga, Dnieper, Volkhov and Neva—are also lacking in meticulous finish. But this crudeness is intentional, for the columns and the figures are meant to be viewed from a distance.

In 1826–1832, warehouses were built on either side of the Exchange (architect I. F. Luchini) which further benefited from the proximity of their plain façades.

The tiered tower of the Kunstkammer and the domed Custom-house on Tuchkov (now Admiral Makarov) Embankment, designed by Luchini, are also perceived as part of the Strelka ensemble, which was further improved by the garden built here by L. A. Ilyin in 1926–1927.

All these buildings now accommodate scientific-research institutes, museums or educational establishments. Thus, the former warehouses are being used by the Zoological Institute and the Zoological Museum, the Dokuchayev Soil Science Museum, and other institutes. The former Custom-house is now occupied by the Institute of Russian Literature of the USSR Academy of Sciences, known as Pushkin House, and the Literary Museum.

Besides the Strelka ensemble, there were other outstanding buildings erected on Vasilyevsky Island early in the 19th century.

One of these is the Mining Institute, built by A. N. Voronikhin in 1806–1811, on the Lt. Schmidt Embankment. This squat, massive building with

Winter stadium (formerly Mikhailovsky manège)

View of the spit (Strelka) of Vasilyevsky Island   Central Naval Museum (formerly the Exchange)

as massive a front portico, adorned with twelve thick columns and two sculptural groups, catches the eye from far away.

Voronikhin, a serf of Count Stroganov, received his freedom when he was already twenty-six years old. His far from easy life was dedicated to tireless creative work, and some of his inspired achievements are ranked among the masterpieces of world architecture. One of these is the Mining Institute. Everything is massive, solid and monumental here: the walls, the portico, the columns and the sculptural groups. The squat, two-storeyed façade stretches along the embankment, but it does not seem too drawn-out because Voronikhin took advantage of a small bend in the river to place his portico there. The portico looks all the more imposing against the absolutely flat walls of the two wings. Twelve well-spaced Doric columns support a huge pediment; a broad open stairway leads up to the portico which indisputably dominates over its surroundings.

The sculptural groups, set far apart on each side of the stairway, symbolise the earth, its power and its wealth. "Hercules and Antaeus" is the work of S. S. Pimenov. Antaeus's strength lay in his contact with Mother-earth, and Hercules only defeated him by severing this contact. Pimenov depicts that moment in the struggle of the two titans when Hercules finally succeeds in lifting Antaeus in the air. For his group, V. Demut-Malinovsky also turned to mythology and chose the story of Proserpina's abduction by Pluto. Once again the figures are shown in desperate struggle, and their dynamism makes a sharp contrast to the stolid imperturbability of the massive portico and the long, plain walls. These figures, and the building as a whole, are meant to be viewed from across the Neva.

Simultaneously with the Mining Institute a building that was fated to play the main role in shaping the city's architectural centre, was going up on the opposite bank of the Neva, a little further upstream. This was the Admiralty (1806–1823), the inspired creation of A. D. Zakharov, and one of the more outstanding monuments of Russian national architecture.

The graceful silhouette of the Admiralty's spire, which has long become the emblem of the city and which adorns the medal "For the Defence of Leningrad," is familiar to everybody, even people who had never been to Leningrad. When you come out into the square in front of Moscow Station or the embankment in front of Warsaw Station, the first thing you see is the spire of the Admiralty shining in the distance. However much you may admire the architecture, the embankments and the squares, you will always remember this unique spire as one of Leningrad's finest adornments.

Reading Pushkin's lines you feel that for him the Admiralty spire was an inseparable part of St. Petersburg and its white nights:

> *When in my room I write or read,*
> *No lamp or candle do I need.*
> *In streets deserted mansions sleep,*
> *And o'er their clearly etched outlines*
> *The Admiralty Needle shines ...*

Zakharov erected his building on the site of the old Admiralty fortress and shipyard, designed by Peter the Great himself, and built in 1704. According to the rules of fortification, a large space had been cleared in front of the earthworks. As a fortress, the Admiralty soon lost its significance, but the yard was used for building and repairing ships for a hundred years longer. In the seventeen-thirties, workshops designed by architect I. K. Korobov were built round the yard in a broad letter "U" with an entrance arch in the centre, adorned with a small turret and spire. When P. M. Yeropkin planned the layout of the Neva's left bank, he saw the three principal streets converging on this spire. As the city's centre began to take shape in close proximity to the Admiralty it became increasingly clear that Korobov's plain utility buildings had to be reconstructed from scratch. The job was given to Zakharov, then a professor of the Academy of Arts. He submitted his design for the radical reconstruction of the Admiralty in 1806. He kept the old layout of the building, some of the walls and the spire, which he used for the compositional pivot of the whole edifice, but he designed his own façades and interiors.

There are two parallel buildings linked at the Neva end by arched pavillions forming a broad "U" as in the old Admiralty. In the past, canals

One of the Rostral columns

Sculpture on the Rostral column

Sculpture on the Rostral column

connecting the shipyard with the river, ran under these arches. Korobov's idea of making two separate buildings was not renounced by Zakharov because in those years of reconstruction the Admiralty performed two different functions as the naval administration and the shipyard. The Naval Ministry, formed in 1805, was housed here in the building facing the city, and the workshops were in the one at the back.

The Admiralty is a huge edifice with the main façade stretching for 406 metres, and two 163-metre long side façades. The problem of relieving the monotony of these long walls was solved by Zakharov with great success. Rejecting the obvious solution of using an abundance of ornaments, he achieved the desired effect by finding the best proportions and a rhythmical alternation of the separate parts of the building. He divided the endless main façade into three parts with a massive cube supporting a graceful tiered tower in the centre, and each of the other two parts symmetrically decorated with three porticoes of six, twelve and six columns. The wall space between the central cube and the first of the porticos has far-spaced windows framed in modest platbands. By skilfully combining
these simple elements, Zakharov attains an impression of palatial grandeur.

The side façades repeat the three-portico pattern with the same number of columns. The length of the building, emphasised by the prevalence of horizontal lines, corresponds to the spaciousness of the city squares around it, dominated by the spired tower, which is reminiscent of ancient Russian churches and kremlins in design. The massive central cube with an arched drive-in is topped by another cube almost half its size adorned with 28 Ionic columns, and the next tier is the lantern of the dome, gradually narrowing to form the spire, crowned with a weathervane in the shape of a caravel. The tower together with the spire is 72.5 metres high. The top part, as designed by Korobov, has remained almost unchanged, and the skeleton of the old tower has been kept inside the new one, as in a case.

In his design, Zakharov freely combined elements of classicism with the early eighteenth century style of architecture. While relying on the order systems in the main, and while striving for the utmost clarity of composition, he nevertheless introduced the spire, a startlingly vertical element

Institute of Russian Literature under the USSR
Academy of Sciences (formerly the Custom-
house)

"Hercules and Antaeus" at the entrance to the
Mining Institute

Mining Institute

rudely disrupting the smooth flow of the horizontal lines, in the manner of the spires in Peter the Great's reign. Zakharov creatively assimilated all the past architectural experience and produced the only building of its kind where every detail speaks of a great master's unique individuality.

Sculpture plays an essential role in the Admiralty building. When drawing up his design Zakharov did not merely mark the location of the sculptural decorations but also their subject matter. On the façade there are 56 statues, 11 large reliefs and 350 mouldings. The synthesis of sculpture and architecture, so typical for Russian 19th century classicism, is nowhere as pronounced as in the Admiralty building. Eminent Russian sculptors Shchedrin, Terebenev, Demut-Malinovsky and Pimenov worked on the decorations. Unfortunately, not all of them have survived. In 1860, when one of the wings was converted into a church, Alexander II ordered all the statues, except the ones in the central part of the building, to be removed. In fulfilling this barbarous order twenty-two statues of rare artistic value were destroyed.

Only the central tower has been fully preserved. The haut relief over the arched drive-in (sculptor I. I. Terebenev) is the main one, both thematically and compositionally, and is dedicated to the consolidation of the Russian navy which the sculptor glorifies in allegorical figures. There is Neptune presenting Peter the Great with a trident—the symbol of Russia's power over the sea; under a bay tree nearby stands the figure of a young woman personifying Russia, holding cornucopia and leaning on the club of Hercules. There are also Minerva, Mercury and Vulcan, glorifying Russia and Peter the Great, and a little apart is the winged figure of Glory, carrying the Russian flag over the ocean sailed by ships of the new navy, surrounded by sea nymphs. This intricate composition, apart from its excellent execution, is cleverly linked with the other sculptural decorations.

Haut reliefs depicting the winged deities of Glory carrying the banners of victory (sculptor Terebenev) are placed directly above the arch, and on either side of the entrance stand monumental groups of sea nymphs, supporting globes (sculptor F. F. Shchedrin). Each group symbolises the mythological goddess Hecate in her three shapes. The white figures look

View of the Admiralty from St. Isaac's Cathedral

impressively strong and dignified against the smooth yellow walls. The figures of four classical heroes—Achilles, Ajax, Pyrrhus and Alexander the Great—placed on the top corners of the lower, massive cube, soften the transition to the contrastingly lightweight cube above. The figures set above each of the 28 columns surrounding this second cube allegorically represent the four seasons of the year, the four elements—water, earth, air and fire, the four winds, Isis, the patroness of seafaring, and Urania, the goddess of astronomy. These figures in their turn soften the transition to the lantern of the dome, ending in the spire.

Of particular interest among the sculptural decorations of the other sections of the building are Terebenev's reliefs on the pediments of the side porticoes called: "Themis crowning achievements of artists," "Themis giving rewards for victories on land and sea," "Glory crowning war feats" and "Glory crowning learing."

Almost all the sculpture decorating the Admiralty is connected with seafaring and shipbuilding and renders in images the leitmotif of the whole construction; glory to Russia, a great sea power!

Of the halls that have been preserved intact, mention must be made first of all of the main vestibule with its wide staircase at the foot of which are two large seated figures of Heracles and Pallas Athena (sculptor Terebenev). An arcade runs round the vestibule, and above it rises the rectangular double colonnade of the main floor. Inspite of its severe forms, the vestibule looks bright and cheerful.

When the Admiralty was first built nothing obscured the view of its main façade: a huge space was cleared in front of it, and Zakharov's masterpiece could also be admired from the Vasilyevsky Island embankment. But all this changed in the eighteen-seventies. The canals connecting the shipyard with the Neva were filled in, an embankment was built between the side pavilions and before long apartment houses began to appear there one after the other, blocking the view from the river. This is an instance of how the city's architectural ensembles were distorted in those last decades of the 19th century.

The Alexandrovsky Garden (since renamed the Gorky Garden) was planted in front of the main façade at that time.

The Admiralty. Main façade

The Admiralty. Main façade

The Admiralty. Sculptural group at the entrance

The Admiralty. Vestibule

During the Great Patriotic War and the siege of Leningrad, a large number of enemy bombs and shells exploded on the territory of the Admiralty, but the damage done to this remarkable historic and artistic monument was quickly repaired by the Leningraders.

The Admiralty unites the city's central squares—the Decembrists' and the Palace Squares.

There are not many squares in world architecture that leave as deep an impression on the viewer as Palace (Dvortsovaya) Square. The amazing sensation of space, the harmony of the buildings surrounding it, and the beauty of each separate building, is all so overwhelming when one first comes into this square, that one cannot sort out one's feelings of admiration at once. Gradually one begins to realise that the secret of this enchantment lies in the integrity of the ensemble, although everything here was built at different times by different architects.

When the Winter Palace, the oldest of the buildings here, was finished the view from its windows was far from attractive—just nondescript houses and waste plots. True, development of the territory in front of the palace began soon afterwards, and in 1779 the boundary of the square was defined by the private houses built in a semi-circle by architect G. Veldten. Still, there was no artistic harmony, and in 1819 Carlo Rossi was commissioned to build a "proper" square in front of the palace. The life of this outstanding architect was wholly bound up with St. Petersburg where he grew up, was educated, worked and died in poverty and obscurity, having been suspended by Nicholas I from participation in any major projects long before his death. Among the ensembles created by Rossi in St. Petersburg, the place of honour belongs to Palace Square.

It was a formidable task designing a building opposite the Winter Palace with Rastrelli's ornate façade stretching the length of the vast square. Rossi's problem was to find the right size and shape for his building so that it would stand up to the palace and harmonise with it. Nor could he forget about the proximity of the Admiralty, built on entirely different artistic principles. And last but not least, he was obliged to continue what Veldten had begun, neither pulling down nor rebuilding anything. Rossi

The Admiralty. Pavilion

solved all these problems brilliantly, and produced one of the finest ensembles in the city.

The enormous white-and-yellow building half-encircling the square is usually called the General Staff. Actually, there are two separate buildings connected by the triumphal arch opposite the main gateway of the Winter Palace. These two buildings with a total frontage of 580 metres were completed in 1829 and were meant to houses the General Staff, the Ministry of Foreign Affairs and the Finance Ministry.

The contrast between the lavishly ornate Winter Palace and the severe General Staff would seem to be too striking, and yet the two edifices are perceived as units of a single ensemble.

The façade of the General Staff is concave in the centre to form the semi-circle. The intentional monotony of the semicircular walls with their endless rows of windows is only slightly relieved by four long balconies. In contrast, the triumphal arch in the centre surpasses nearly all the buildings in the city in magnificence. The arch gives access to the square from Herzen Street (formerly Bolshaya Morskaya) which adjoins it at an angle. In order to make it strictly perpendicular to the main gateway of the Winter Palace, Rossi gave it an artificial curve, boldly spanning it with a seventeen-metre-long double arch at a height of 28 metres.

The Triumphal Arch is decorated with martial figures, winged Glories in haut relief, and various regalia. The crowning point of the composition is the victory chariot on top of the arch (16 m. wide and 10 m. high) designed by eminent Russian sculptors S. S. Pimenov and V. I. Demut-Malinovsky who for many years worked together with Rossi. The six horses, led by two foot soldiers, are harnessed to a chariot in which stands the winged figure of Glory holding the state emblem of Russia in her hand.

The arch seems to be made for the triumphal entrance of victorious troops, and it was in fact, just like the building of the General Staff, erected as a monument to Russia's victory in the war of 1812 with Napoleon. The work of Rossi and his great contemporaries Zakharov, Voronikhin and Stasov, reflects those patriotic feelings and ideas which were so strong in Russian society during this Patriotic War.

Another monument in honour of Russia's victory over Napoleon was

Palace Square

Arch of the General Staff building

Figures of warriors on the arch of the General
Staff building

the Triumphal Column erected in the centre of Palace Square in 1834 (architect A. Montferrand), called the Alexander Column. This is the largest granite monolith in the world. The column is 47.5 metres high–higher than the Vendôme Column in Paris and the Columna Trajana in Rome. Moreover, it is not anchored by anything and is kept secure on the pedestal entirely by its own weight. The whole construction weighs about 600 tons, and the column has a diameter of 3.66 metres. The monolith was hewn out of a cliff in the Puterlak quarry in the vicinity of Vyborg, and brought to St. Petersburg in a specially constructed barge. The column is crowned with the figure of an angel carrying a cross (sculptor B. I. Orlovsky) and trampling on a snake which symbolises the vanquished enemies. The pedestal is ornamented with haut reliefs whose theme is the glory of Russian arms.

In 1837—1843, soon after the erection of the column, a building for the Guards Headquarters was constructed by A. P. Bryullov in the east corner of the square between the Winter Palace and the General Staff. Suited in proportions and style to Rossi's building, it made a good complement to the ensemble.

Later, a cast-iron grille (architect R. Meltser) appeared in front of the Winter Palace and then a rather large glass cupola behind one of the wings of the General Staff, which broke the symmetry of the ensemble. In the nineteen-twenties, the grille was moved to Kirov district (the former Narva Zastava) where it is used as a fence for the Ninth of January Garden. The cobblestone square was asphalted in that same period.

Palace Square was the scene of historical events of decisive importance for Russia, events which also influenced the destinies of mankind in general.

On January 9, 1905, thousands of working people came here from the city's suburbs, carrying icons, religious gonfalons and portraits of the tsar, bringing a petition to His Majesty. The tsarist government prepared its own welcome for this peaceful demonstration. Troops were despatched to all the districts of the city, and martial law was proclaimed. That morning, Palace Square resembled a huge armed camp, with the infantry ranged in the centre, and the cavalry on the flanks, ready to fight back the unarmed workers approaching the square. At about 1. p.m. the troops were ordered

Chariot of Glory. Sculpture on the arch of the
General Staff building

to clear the territory in front of the Winter Palace of people. The cavalry went into attack with drawn swords. They slashed at the workers, and their horses tramped those who had fallen, but still the demonstration was not dispersed. Then the infantry opened fire, shooting point-blank at men, women and children. The square made a gruesome sight. The ground was strewn with dead bodies, the wounded groaned, people screamed and cursed the tsar. There were many children among the killed and the wounded. A similar tragedy occurred in many other parts of the city that day.

The true countenance of tsarism was revealed to the awakened masses by that brutal massacre. January 9 made the beginning of the revolution of 1905. The lesson which the workers were so cruelly taught that day was not forgotten by them, and when they set out for Palace Square again, twelve years later, they carried rifles and machine-guns and not icons. On the historic night of October 25, 1917, armed workers, soldiers and sailors, took the Winter Palace—that last stronghold of the bourgeoisie—by storm.

By early that morning, October 25, nearly all the important points in the city were in the hands of the insurgent people with the exception of the Winter Palace where the Ministers of the bourgeois Provisional Government had gathered in one of the rooms, protected by Cadets. They were waiting for help from their leader Kerensky who had fled in a car belonging to the American Embassy.

When the building was surrounded in a tight circle, an envoy was sent to the Ministers to propose that they should surrender. They refused, and then, at 9.45 p.m., the *Aurora* fired its famous shot (a blank shot it was), giving the signal for attack. The insurgent people advanced on the Winter Palace from different directions: from Millionnaya Street, from the Admiralty, and from the arch of the General Staff. Those entering from the arch had to cross the square where the Cadets defending the Winter Palace had erected barricades from the firewood stacked there and fired at the advancing men. But no power on earth could stem the tide of the revolutionary people. Sweeping aside all the obstacles in their way, they broke into the palace, and fought their way up the stairs and through the rooms until they reached the one where the Ministers of the Provisional Government were ensconced.

Alexander Column

Former Guards Headquarters

In the days following the October armed uprising, Kerensky together with General Krasnov, made an attempt to rally the forces that remained loyal to him and launch an attack on Petrograd. The revolutionary people gave them a shattering rebuff. Lenin himself directed the operations from the Guards Headquarters in Palace Square.

On state and revolutionary holidays a platform is erected here in front of the Winter Palace from which Party and Soviet leaders hail the troop parades and the manifestations of the working people.

The Field of Mars is another important ensemble that took shape in the eighteen-twenties. This largest square in St. Petersburg was called Poteshny (Amusement) Field in the 18th century, and after that—Tsarina's Meadow. In those days it was a park that merged with the Summer Garden. Fêtes with a fireworks display were usually held there, hence the name Poteshny, or Amusement, Field. In the 19th century, however, it was converted into a parade and drill ground and renamed the Field of Mars, after the God of war.

A monument to Field Marshal Suvorov was erected in the south end of the field in 1801. In 1818 it was moved to the north end, nearer the Neva. The sculptor, M. I. Kozlovsky, saw two ways open before him: he could either give Suvorov a portrait likeness and present him as the puny old man he was, or create an allegorical image of a handsome young warrior personifying the glory of Russian arms. He hesitated for a long time before making up his mind. Finally, he chose the second way. There is no portrait likeness between his monument and Suvorov, although a certain resemblance may be discerned in some of the features. The slender figure of the young armour-clad warrior is full of courage and determination, and the sword in his hand is raised to defend his motherland. Suvorov's boundless courage and irrepressible energy are implied, and the inner resemblance is therefore undoubtable.

The round pedestal, probably designed by Kozlovsky and Voronikhin, is adorned with an haut relief by F. G. Gordeyev depicting Glory and Peace crossing a palm and a laurel branch over a shield with an inscription to Suvorov. The small square at the entrance to the Field of Mars from the Kirov Bridge bears the great general's name.

The Field of Mars

Monument to Field Marshal Suvorov

V. P. Stasov played a decisive role in creating the ensemble of the Field of Mars. He built a variety of structures in different parts of St. Petersburg, in Moscow and in other Russian towns. These include triumphal arches, churches, warehouses, stables and barracks. The keynote of all his designs has always been a severe monumentality, and it is best expressed in the Barracks of the Pavlovsky Regiment (now the head office of Lenenergo) on the Field of Mars.

In the 19th century the field was the city's military centre, and Stasov bore this in mind when he took on the assignment of reconstructing the existing buildings on the west side of the square into barracks for the Pavlovsky Regiment. This regiment had distinguished itself in the Patriotic War of 1812, and so, besides serving its practical purpose, the building had to be an architectural embodiment of military valour and glory.

Erected in 1817–1820, the Barracks have certain features in common with both the Admiralty and the General Staff. All three buildings are based on the same patriotic theme, and their long impressive façades seem to symbolise unassailable power. And yet each of them has its own individuality.

The length of the frontage is the first thing one sees in the barracks. Like the Admiralty and the General Staff it stretches for hundreds of metres with a pronounced prevalence of horizontal divisions. The frontage facing the Field of Mars is decorated with Doric porticoes—a twelve-column one in the centre, and two six-column porticoes at the ends of the building. The widely spaced columns of the central portico support a heavy, tiered attic decorated with regimental colours and arms in haut relief. The pediments supported by the end porticoes are perfectly plain, thus accentuating the grandeur of the central one.

The rhythmical alternation of the identical sections, the straight lines and severe planes of this long façade give that impression of "uniform beauty" which Pushkin spoke of, recalling the military parades he had watched in the Field of Mars.

The interior is efficiently simple, as required by the purpose of the building.

The Barracks occupies most of the west side of the field and while pro-

Monument to the heroes of the Revolution

portionately conforming to the buildings which had stood here before it determined, in its turn, the character of the later structures put up beside it. This is most apparent in the Land Department built by architect Adamini in the adjoining lot.

In spite of the splendour of the Marble Palace, the Engineers' Castle and the Barracks, the field itself remained an unattractive drill ground until 1917.

In March 1917, after the overthrow of the autocracy, the heroes of the February revolution who had fallen in battle were buried in the centre of the field. The funeral developed into a great manifestation, which started the tradition of holding mass meetings and demonstrations at these common graves. In April 1917, the working people gathered here for a meeting of protest against the imperialistic policy of the Provisional Government. On May 1, Lenin addressed the working people who had gathered on the Field of Mars to celebrate this day of international solidarity. A mass demonstration took place here on June 18 (July 1, New Style). All the political parties in Russia made preparations for this meeting which had to show which party had more followers among the proletariat of Petrograd. The masses clearly demonstrated their allegiance to the Bolshevik party whose slogans were inscribed on more than ninety per cent of all the banners carried that day. The meeting showed how greatly the prestige of the Communist Party had grown among the proletariat of Petrograd.

In the years that followed, the Field of Mars remained an honourable place of burial. Buried here, beside the heroes of the February revolution, are heroes of the Civil War and prominent leaders of the Communist Party—M. S. Uritsky, V. Volodarsky, N. G. Tolmachev, A. S. Rakov, I. I. Gaza and others.

In 1917–1919, a granite tomb was designed by architect L. V. Rudnev. It consists of low stone blocks which form a tiered rectangle with passages left open on every side leading to the centre. Epitaphs, composed by A. V. Lunacharsky (the first People's Commissar of Education) are inscribed on each of the eight solid blocks placed at the sides of the four entrances. One of them reads:

The names of all the heroes
Who shed their blood for freedom
Are unknown.
Humanity reveres the nameless,
And in their honour,
In memory of all of them
This stone has been erected
To stand here for all time . . .

The tomb is unconventional in its artistic design—just the low stone slabs instead of the usual carved figure or obelisk. The design is justified, however, by the location of the graves in the middle of the field. An obelisk, however big, would look unimpressive and insignificant here, whereas the horizontal slabs appear to be the best solution to the problem of bringing out the centre of this vast, flat field.

Erecting these monuments to the heroes of the Revolution was the first step in reconstructing the field. In 1920, Petrograders turned out in their thousands for a mass *subbotnik* in honour of May Day, to transform the unkempt drill ground into a garden. Before long the field became unrecognizable: straight walks radiated from the tomb with diagonal paths crossing them; there were green lawns between them adorned with shrubs and flower beds; on three sides the field was surrounded with a hedge of trimmed limes. Architect I. A. Fomin was in charge of the reconstruction and planting of the Field of Mars which, together with the neighbouring Summer and Mikhailovsky gardens—made a beautiful green spot in the very heart of the city.

That winter of 1941—42, the first grim winter of war, trenches and dugouts scarred this field, and when spring came it was planted with potatoes and vegetables which were vitally needed by the Leningraders during the enemy blockade.

Today, the Field of Mars has been given back its pre-war look. It makes a beautiful sight, when viewed from Kirov Bridge, with its green lawns, neat walks, the darker green of the parks behind it, the dark-red bulk of the Engineers' Castle with its gleaming golden spire in the background, and the yellow-and-white façades of the Barracks to the right.

In November 1957, on the fortieth anniversary of the Great October Socialist Revolution, an eternal fire was lighted in the centre of the square before the graves of the heroes of the Revolution.

Pushkin Theatre of Drama. Main façade

In that period when the sumptuous ensembles were taking shape on the banks of the Neva, construction of Nevsky Prospekt–the city's main thoroughfare–was also begun.

The Nevsky developed in stages: first, it was a path cut through the woods to connect the Admiralty shipyards with the Moscow road, the Alexander Nevsky Lavra and the Smolny Dvor; later it became known as the Nevsky "Perspective Road" where palaces rubbed shoulders with low, timber hovels; and in mid-eighteenth century it began to acquire its present status of the city's main thoroughfare.

Gogol begins his story "Nevsky Prospekt" with the following words: "There is nothing better than Nevsky Prospekt, in St. Petersburg at any rate; it means everything for this city. What doesn't this beauty-street of our capital excel in?"

The Nevsky became especially handsome after the appearance of the ensembles and squares designed by Voronikhin and Rossi.

If you start down this four-and-a-half-kilometre long street from the

Nevsky Prospekt

Admiralty you will not be particularly impressed at first. It will seem just a street like any other, not too wide and not too handsome, with some houses better-looking than others. But as soon as you cross the Moika you will find that the street becomes wider, the buildings more varied and interesting, and a little further on the solid line of houses on the right-hand side will break off abruptly to give way to a square on which towers the Kazan Cathedral, built by Voronikhin in 1801–1811.

A semi-circular court is formed in front of the cathedral by its majestic yet graceful colonnade which faces the Nevsky. Paul I, who ordered the building of the Kazan Cathedral, demanded that it should be modelled on the Cathedral of St. Peter in Rome with its open colonnade. Voronikhin's approach, however, was entirely original and his design differed in many respects from that of the Roman cathedral. There, the colonnade is much smaller than the portico with which it is hardly connected. Voronikhin's colonnade is of the same height as the portico and seems to branch out from the body of the cathedral itself. In Rome, the colonnade forms a closed circle round the inner court, and here the end walls are turned to Nevsky Prospekt, linking it with the adjoining streets.

In designing the building Voronikhin had to solve a number of difficult problems. One of these was that, by tradition, the altar had to face east, and so the main façade would face a side street and not the Nevsky. He found a bold solution to this problem by building the colonnade before the Nevsky façade, and looking at it one forgets that it is not the main façade. This majestic colonnade consisting of four rows of Corinthian columns ends in wide arches over the side streets.

Voronikhin planned to build a similar colonnade on the opposite side of the cathedral, but the outbreak of the war of 1812 prevented him from carrying his idea into effect.

The colonnade conceals most of the cathedral building, and only the tall cupola rises above the columns in the centre. The length of the colonnade is excellently balanced by the height of the cupola (70 metres).

The cathedral building is shaped like a cross, and the walls are decorated with Corinthian pilasters and deep, large windows. Tall statues of Prince Vladimir and Alexander Nevsky (sculptor Pimenov), St. Andrew (sculptor Prokofiev) and John the Baptist (sculptor Martos) stand in the niches behind the columns. The sculptors who decorated the cathedral followed the general idea of the architect, which is evidenced by the figures in front of the porticoes and the haut reliefs on the side attics of the colonnade, the one on the eastern side showing Moses striking water from a stone (I. P. Martos) and the other, on the western side, depicting the *Copper Serpent* (I. P. Prokofiev). These skilfully executed complex compositions underlining the length of the attics are best viewed from afar.

Inside, the cathedral little resembles the usual churches with their massive pylons supporting heavy, vaulted ceilings. It is light and elegant, and is more like a palace than a cathedral. The pylons are so slender that their structural strength was questioned at first. The general impression of solemnity is produced by the 56 monolithic columns with bases and Corinthian capitals made of bronze.

The construction is also interesting from the engineering point of view. The diameter of the cupola exceeds 17 metres, and in designing it Voronikhin introduced a bold innovation by using iron and cast iron. His engineering competence is also proved by the construction of the arches at the two ends of the colonnade. They have a span of approximately 7 metres, and doubt was voiced by many at the time of construction whether the columns would be able to support the weight. All these fears proved unfounded: Voronikhin's design was irreproachable both technically and artistically.

The graceful cast-iron grille in front of the western façade was supposed to link the ends of the two colonnades (the one on the opposite side of the building did not materialise) and form a small square before the main entrance to the cathedral.

In 1813, soon after the completion of the building, the remains of Field

Kazan Cathedral

Kazan Cathedral. Interior   Grille of Kazan Cathedral

Marshal Kutuzov were ceremoniously transferred to the cathedral, where captured enemy colours, keys to enemy cities taken by Russian armies in the war against Napoleon, and other war mementos were deposited.

Monuments to Kutuzov and Barclay de Tolly (sculptor B. I. Orlovsky) were erected in front of the cathedral and unveiled in 1837. A better place could hardly be found for these monuments which further stress the memorial significance of the cathedral. Their silhouettes stand out clearly against the end arches of the colonnade, harmonising with the columns in proportions. Kutuzov and Barclay de Tolly are dressed in the 1812 uniforms of Russian generals, and their portrait likeness is excellent. In one hand Kutuzov holds a lowered sword and in the other—his field marshal's baton. He seems to be slowly moving forward and his firm step, confident gestures and his whole figure breathe the calm of invincible strength.

The statue of Barclay de Tolly is more static. He seems to have paused in reflection, with a preoccupied and even stern expression on his face. With his right hand he is holding up his cape, and his left hand, in which he has the field marshal's baton is drawn slightly back.

The pronounced dissimilarity of the two men's characters does not upset the harmony of the monuments at all.

The square formed by the colonnade facing Nevsky Prospekt was the site of many revolutionary demonstrations. One of the most memorable was the demonstration of December 6 (November 18) 1876 where a speech was made by G. V. Plekhanov, one of the first disseminators of Marxism in Russia. It was the first time that workers took part in a mass political action.

A garden, adorned with a fountain, was laid out in front of the cathedral in 1900. A fountain designed by architect Thomas de Thomon which since 1809 had stood on the road to Tsarskoye Selo was moved here and installed in front of the western façade, in the centre of the semi-circle formed by Voronikhin's grille.

ФЕЛЬДМАРШАЛУ
КНЯЗЮ
КУТУЗОВУ СМОЛЕНСКОМУ
1812

Monument to Field Marshal Kutuzov

Monument to Field Marshal Barclay de Tolly

The Kazan Cathedral now houses the Museum of the History of Religion and Atheism.

Continuing down Nevsky Prospekt you will soon come to Brodsky Street, branching off to the left, and see a palace in the distance. If you come closer, you will see a square, with a lawn in the centre, lined with severely uniform buildings. There would seem to be little attraction in these plain yellow walls, and yet you are enchanted the moment you enter this square. The uniform rows of windows, the laconism of the straight lines, and the severity of these façades make a wonderful prelude for the radiant beauty of the palace at the end of the square.

This palace was built by Carlo Rossi in 1819–1825 for the Grand Duke Mikhail on a large site between the Nevsky, the rivers Moika and Fontanka, and the Yekaterininsky Canal. When designing the palace, Rossi rearranged and reconstructed the whole of the surrounding district so thoroughly that it became quite unrecognizable.

The Mikhailovsky Palace was highly admired by contemporaries who thought it one of the finest buildings in St. Petersburg.

As always with Rossi, the composition is logical and clear-cut. The central part of the building is taller and more ornate than the two smaller, adjoining wings. A Corinthian portico of eight columns, set upon a ground-floor arcade, makes the centre of the main façade. To the right and left of the portico, the second storey of the building is adorned with Corinthian semi-columns placed between the large oval windows. Sculpture has been used lavishly. Bronze lions guard the broad staircase leading to the main entrance; the flat walls above the ground-floor windows are decorated with lions' heads and coats-of-arms; and an ornament in haut relief runs along the length of the façade on a level with the capitals of the semi-columns.

A park was laid out behind the palace where the façade is just as splendid as the main one. Here, twelve Corinthian columns form a wide loggia with a decorative attic. The white columns, yellow walls, and the lush green of the park combine into a truly lovely picture.

Brodsky Street

The interior of the palace produced a staggering effect. Besides being an excellent architect Rossi was also a remarkable interior decorator, and he made the drawings for most of the furniture and ornaments himself. Working in cooperation with him were sculptor Demut-Malinovsky, painters John and Peter Scotti, Barnaba Medici, Yakov and Vasily Dodonov, and the town's best upholsterers, carvers, carpenters and cabinet-makers. The main vestibule and staircase and the White Hall on the main floor have been preserved intact, despite all the alterations made in the palace since.

The vestibule somewhat resembles that of the Admiralty, but it is more ornate and resplendent. On entering it, one first becomes aware of its spaciousness and height. A broad staircase leads to the main floor with columns decorating the gallery.

Columns divide the White Hall into three parts. The elaborate Corinthian capitals, gilded cornices, ceiling paintings and picturesque wall panels, make this a very ornate room.

In 1895, the palace was made into a museum and the interior was almost completely re-arranged. A new building, which now houses the Ethnographical Museum of the Peoples of the USSR, came to replace the side wing.

Today, the Mikhailovsky Palace is occupied by the State Russian Museum which is one of the country's largest depositories of Russian national art. Displayed there are the paintings of Levitsky, Bryullov, Fedotov, Repin, Surikov, Serov, the works of sculptors Rastrelli, Shubin, Antokolsky, and other outstanding works of art. Modern Soviet artists are also well represented.

Simultaneously with the construction of the Mikhailovsky Palace, improvements were made to the surrounding area. A rectangular square called the Mikhailovsky Square (since renamed Arts Square) was designed by Rossi in front of the main façade with a severely plain high iron grille railing off the formal front court. Two new streets—Engineers' (Inzhenernaya) and Sadovaya—were laid to make the southern and eastern boundaries of

"Lazarus Raised from the Dead", Rublev, 15th
century (Russian Museum)

Russian Museum (formerly Mikhailovsky Palace).
Main façade

Monument to Alexander Pushkin

the palace grounds. Later, a third street, also called Mikhailovskaya and since renamed Brodsky, was laid to connect the palace with Nevsky Prospekt from where the central portico could be viewed.

As a result, the Mikhailovsky Palace became the centre of a large ensemble. When planning the large square in front of the palace, Rossi also made designs for the dwelling houses to be built there eventually.

Rossi did not erect them himself, but the architects who did used his designs. They were not "dwelling houses" however. One of them was the Mikhailovsky Theatre built by A. P. Bryullov in 1831–1833, and without knowing this story one is dismayed by the contrast between the plain, dwelling house exterior and the lavishly decorated interior. On second thought one realises that putting in a sumptuous theatrical entrance would spoil the architectural harmony of the whole square.

The Mikhailovsky Theatre has been renamed the Maly Theatre of Opera and Ballet which has earned repute for its productions of Soviet operas and ballets. Its work has been rewarded with the Order of Lenin.

Architect Paul Jacot, like Bryullov, also used Rossi's design for the Dvoryanskoye Sobraniye (Noblemen's Club) which he built on the corner of the square and Mikhailovskaya Street, and which is now occupied by the Leningrad Philharmonic Society. Other architects who built up the square followed the example of Bryullov and Jacot. However, this ensemble, which included the palace, the square, and Mikhailovskaya Street lined on both sides with practically identical buildings, was upset in the second half of the 19th century. In the eighteen-seventies, when a storey was added to one of these houses bought for an hotel, the façade was completely re-decorated without any regard for the surrounding buildings. As little consideration was given to the ensemble when a building opposite was made over for the Volga-Kama Bank in 1898.

In 1946–1948, its original appearance, distorted in the period of capitalist development, was restored. Restoration work was done on the building of the Philharmonic Society, the garden in the centre of the square was

"Italian Noonday", Bryullov

"A Merchant's Wife", Kustodiev

"Shrovetide", Kustodiev

re-planted since the trees blocked the view of the palace from Nevsky Prospekt, and the façades of the school built by architect N. A. Trotsky on the east side of the square were remodelled to fit in with the rest of the ensemble.

A monument to Pushkin erected in the centre of the square by sculptor M. K. Anikushin with the pedestal by architect V. A. Petrov was unveiled in June 1957. The four-metre tall bronze figure of Pushkin stands on a tetrahedral pedestal. His gesture and his whole attitude are youthfully impulsive, and he seems to be reciting his inspired poetry before a rapt audience. The monument blends admirably with the ensemble.

M. K. Anikushin worked for more than ten years on this monument which brought him a Lenin Prize and which is acclaimed one of the finest in Leningrad.

On the other side of Nevsky Prospekt, not far from Arts Square, there is another architectural ensemble—perhaps the best of Rossi's creations. It is known as the Alexandrinsky Theatre ensemble which includes two squares and the street between them. The Ostrovsky Square opens on to the Nevsky from where a good view can be had of the main façade of the theatre.

The well balanced proportions of the different units, the masterful choice of sculptural decorations, and its harmony with the surrounding houses, make this theatre a remarkable piece of architecture. Its majestic simplicity brings Rossi's artistic credo to mind: "The aim is not abundance of decoration, but majesty of form and nobility of proportion." The plain yellow walls make a good background for the white six-column loggia in the centre of the main façade, the white haut-relief decorations and the statues of the Muses. The designation of this building is obvious: in niches, on either side of the loggia raised above the ground floor, stand the figures of Terpsichore, the Muse of dancing, and Melpomene, the Muse of tragedy; a lyre in a laurel wreath adorns the attic of the loggia, crowned with a chariot of Apollo, the patron of the arts (by sculptor S. S. Pimenov). The whole building is girdled with a frieze of theatrical masks and garlands. The rear façade is decorated with pilasters and also the figures of Clio, the Muse of history, and Euterpe, the Muse of music and lyric poetry.

The statues designed by Triscorni were removed soon after the completion of the building, and it was not until a century later that they were put back in place. The existing figures are copies of the originals made by I. V. Krestovsky (Terpsichore), D. N. Malashkin (Melpomene), S. A. Yevseyev (Clio) and N. V. Mikhailov (Euterpe).

The interior is a riot of gilt and carving depicting helmets, shields, armour and just intricately designed ornaments. The upper galleries are less resplendent.

From the engineering point of view, Rossi's building was one of the most progressive in his day, and his ideas had a large influence on the theatrical architecture of the subsequent decades.

The Pushkin Drama Theatre, as the Alexandrinsky Theatre has been renamed, is the oldest one in Leningrad. Among the celebrated actors and actresses who played on its stage we can name Martynov, Sosnitsky, Savina, Strepetova, Varlamov, Davydov, Yurie, Korchagina-Alexandrovskaya, Cherkasov, Simonov, Tolubeyev, Borisov and Merkuriev. The theatre has received the Order of the Red Banner, a high Government award, and a replica of the order adorns the façade.

Ostrovsky Square, as we have already said, is part of the ensemble designed by Rossi, who also built the two small pavilions of the Anichkov Palace bordering on the eastern side of the square. The Saltykov-Shchedrin Public Library frames the square on the western side.

The Public Library on the corner of Nevsky Prospekt and Sadovaya Street was built in the seventeen-nineties by architect Y. T. Sokolov. Both in size and in appearance the building was well suited to its purpose, but as the library's collections grew the need for larger premises became imperative. The additional block fronting on Ostrovsky Square was built by Rossi in 1828—1832 at the same time as the Alexandrinsky Theatre. A not very deep Ionic loggia stretches almost the entire length of the façade, with alabaster figures of ancient philosophers and poets (sculptors Demut-Malinovsky, Pimenov, Galberg, Tokarev, Krylov and Leppe) placed between the columns. Crowning the building is a statue of Athena, the goddess of wisdom, by Demut-Malinovsky.

Lenin was a regular reader of this library from 1893 to 1895. Ivan Krylov, the fabulist, and V. V. Stasov, the eminent critic, worked there for many long years. It is the second largest book depository in the Soviet Union (the largest being the Lenin Library in Moscow), containing approximately fourteen million books and also many rare and extremely valuable editions and documents. Several thousand people use the library every day and now it has spread over to the adjoining buildings and also the former Yekaterininsky Boarding School built by Quarenghi on the Fontanka embankment.

In 1873, a monument to Catherine II designed by artist M. O. Mikeshin was unveiled in the centre of the square fronted by the Alexandrinsky Theatre and the Public Library. The empress, wearing her ceremonial robes and holding a sceptre and a wreath in her hand stands on a high, round pedestal at the base of which are grouped the most distinguished figures of late-eighteenth century Russia—Suvorov, Rumyantsev, Potemkin, Orlov, Chichagov, Bezborodko, Betskoi, Derzhavin and Dashkova.

Mikeshin's design was executed by two eminent sculptors—M. A. Chizhov, who made the figure of Catherine II, and A. M. Opekushin who worked on the figures for the base. Mikeshin's restricting solemnly-static composition prevented these sculptors from fully revealing their skill. It was demanded of them that such external details as the folds of the empress's robe and the decorations on the uniforms of the generals should be rendered with meticulous care, but the characters of the people portrayed were not brought out, and because of this the otherwise imposing monument leaves the viewer unimpressed. What is more, its pyramidal shape rather interferes with the view of the theatre from Nevsky Prospekt.

Simultaneously with the ensemble in Ostrovsky Square, Rossi built a new street behind the theatre, leading to the Fontanka and ending in a small semi-circular square. A number of old buildings had to be pulled down and the whole of that district planned anew. The new street was only 220 metres long and 22 metres wide, and the houses were also 22 metres high. These well-balanced proportions and the classical beauty of the street made it a real masterpiece of urban architecture. The identical houses lining the street on both sides make an artistic whole with the rear façade of the theatre and the buildings on the square near the Fontanka.

The street looks its best from this square. A recurring pattern of twin white semi-columns and large windows above the high plinth floor continues down the length of this street. This quiet rhythm is in full accord with the buildings that complete the ensemble. In order to offset the importance of the theatre, Rossi used the Doric order and simplified the design of the ornament as for as he could. His initial plan was to build the plinth floor as an open arcade of small shops, but on hearing about this the eminent Gostiny Dvor merchants sent a petition to the tsar begging him to protect them from this threatened competition. Their appeal was satisfied, and Rossi was compelled to give up the idea of the arcade.

At the head of Chernyshev Street (now Lomonosov Street) Rossi built a three-span arch (the middle one a sham). Later, in the eighteen-nineties, a bust of Mikhail Lomonosov, the great Russian scientist whose name the square now bears, was installed in the centre of this square. The sculptor was P. P. Zabello.

Although the ensemble envisaged by Rossi in the region of Ostrovsky and Lomonosov Squares did not fully materialise, what he did achieve speaks of the consummate skill with which he solved the most difficult problems of urban construction. The street he designed, which joins Ostrovsky and Lomonosov Squares and which was originally called Teatralnaya, has been renamed Rossi Street.

Beyond Ostrovsky Square, the Nevsky goes past the Anichkov Palace

Pavilion in Mikhailovsky Garden

Rossi Pavilion in Ostrovsky Square

and crosses the Fontanka over the small Anichkov Bridge which is widely known from pictures, post cards, drawings and photographs. The bridge owes its popularity to sculptor Klodt's horses, the masterpiece which brought him world-wide fame. There are four different groups representing a youth taming a mettlesome horse. Klodt made the first two groups in 1841 and himself cast them in bronze. One of them shows a youth holding back the horse with a strong hand, and the other—a youth checking a rearing horse. Each of the groups was cast twice, and the four of them were set up at the four corners of the bridge. Shortly afterwards one of the pairs was removed by order of Nicholas I and sent to Berlin as a gift, where the groups were installed in front of the King's palace. A few years later, the other pair was also given away as a gift, and set up in Naples at the entrance to the royal gardens. Anichkov Bridge was temporarily left with plaster models of the originals, and in 1849–1850 Klodt cast two new groups that were even more dynamic and expressive. In one of them, the rearing horse has almost broken free, but the youth crouching on the ground, with the reins twisted round his arm, manages to hold it back. In the other group, the struggle continues. The youth is compelled to fall on one knee for a better grip and pull the reins tight. He has strong arms and he seems confident of finally taming the wild horse.

The four different groups are parts of a single sculptural composition that is splendidly integrated into the general panorama of Nevsky Prospekt.

The stretch of Nevsky Prospekt from the Admiralty to Anichkov Bridge is especially notable for its architectural monuments. Further on, one sees ordinary dwelling houses, most of them built in late nineteenth-early twentieth centuries.

Needless to say, the banks of the Neva and Nevsky Prospekt are not the only places in Leningrad where early nineteenth century architecture and sculpture can be seen. Structures erected in that period will, be found in different parts of the town, and some of them deserve close study. For instance, the Narva Gate, a triumphal arch in honour of Russia's victory over

Napoleon built in the south-west part of the town, on the road by which the victorious Russian armies returned from Paris.

Originally, in 1814, the arch was made of wood by Quarenghi, but then it was decided to keep this monument to Russian military glory, and in 1831—1834 V. P. Stasov was commissioned to build a stone arch, in place of the wooden one, maintaining the old design but using a larger scale.

The classically severe brick arch is faced with sheets of copper. Statues of warriors in old Russian armour stand between the tall twin columns, and crowning the arch is a Chariot of Glory pulled by six galloping horses. The group was made by three eminent sculptors: P. K. Klodt (horses), V. I. Demut-Malinovsky (chariot), and S. S. Pimenov (Glory), and is more dynamic than the chariot crowning the General Staff. The arch is further adorned with statues of Glory and Victory, and haut-relief winged geniuses carrying wreaths. The names of towns and villages where the Russian armies distinguished themselves in decisive battles are carved on the gates. Borodino, Tarutino, Maloyaroslavets, Krasnoye, Leipzig, Paris—the milestones on the hard but glorious road traversed by Kutuzov's armies.

The Narva triumphal arch was badly damaged in the last war, and now it has been fully restored. It stands in Stachki (Strikes) Square—the centre of a new, modern neighbourhood that has grown up here in place of the old Narvskaya Zastava (Narva Gate), once a slum with muddy roads and hovels.

A site of interest on Moscovsky Prospekt, in the southern part of town, is the Moscow triumphal arch made of cast-iron to the design of V. P. Stasov, and installed here in 1834—1838 in honour of Russia's victories over Turkey. A heavy roof is supported by twelve massive Doric columns placed in two rows, but thanks to its fine proportions the gate, on the whole, does not seem too ponderous. The construction was dismantled at one time, and not restored until 1959.

Other early nineteenth century buildings worth seeing include the Yelagin Palace, built by Rossi on Yelagin Island, and set in gardens which are now known as the Kirov Recreation Park. Not far away, on Kamenny Ostrov,

Saltykov-Shchedrin Public Library. Main façade   Saltykov-Shchedrin Public Library. View from
the Fontanka

Sculpture on the attic of the Saltykov-Shchedrin
Public Library

Cicero, by sculptor Krylov   Hippocrates, by sculptor Demut-Malinovsky

Euripides, by sculptor Galberg   Homer, by sculptor Pimenov

Plato, by sculptor Pimenov

there is the interesting wooden building of the Theatre (architect S. Shustov) whose main attraction is the magnificent eight-column portico. In that same period V. P. Stasov built the Trinity (Troitsky) and Transfiguration (Preobrazhensky) Cathedrals on Izmailovsky Prospekt and Pestel Street respectively, and designed the former royal stables between Konyushennaya Square and the Moika.

The creations of Zakharov, Voronikhin, Rossi and Stasov were the acknowledged masterpieces of nineteenth century Russian classicism. The edifices and ensembles designed by them remain unsurpassed and are the pride of Russian architecture. Everything that was built in St. Petersburg in the subsequent decades of the 19th century is much inferior, and this also applies to St. Isaac's Cathedral—the largest of the mid-nineteenth century edifices.

Its golden dome, like the spires of the Peter and Paul Fortress and the Admiralty, is seen from afar. The very size of the dome, raised to a great height, makes one imagine the size of the cathedral itself. Indeed, it is much larger than all the other churches in the city and can admit more than twelve thousand people at a time.

Coming close to the cathedral, one does not know what to look at first: the gleaming dome, the polished granite columns, the gray marble facing of the walls, the ornamented doors, or the sculptural groups on the pediments. The sight of all this splendour makes one pause to think of the skill of the artists who decorated this building, and the toil of those thousands of workers who erected it.

Many-columned porticoes surround the square building on all four sides. The main, beautifully shaped dome, which is a definite asset to the city's skyline, is surrounded by four smaller domes. All the other elements of the building are also very good in themselves. But when one looks at the cathedral as a whole, one involuntarily thinks, after the first staggering sensation has subsided: aren't there too many ornaments? There are statues, haut reliefs, columns, marble, gold-plating everywhere. For all its ornateness,

Monument to Catherine II

Rossi Street

Lomonosov Square and Lomonosov Street

Bust of Lomonosov

Anichkov Bridge

the great stone bulk of the cathedral has none of Rastrelli's graceful picturesqueness; rather the contrary, its over-ornateness makes the massive building more cumbersome still. The separate elements are not well balanced and they might have been more proportionate to one another. For instance, the statues at the corners are too big, the reliefs on the pediments too heavy, and the five domes are not properly correlated. Therefore, with all due credit given for its separate elements, the cathedral as a whole can hardly be ranked with the best in Russian classical architecture.

This edifice was designed by A. Montferrand who came to Russia in 1816, and shortly afterwards entered the competition for the best design of the cathedral. In his anxiety to please all tastes, Montferrand presented his design in 24 different variants, one of which was approved by Alexander I,

Anichkov Bridge. Equestrian group

Anichkov Bridge. Equestrian group

Anichkov Bridge. Equestrian group

Anichkov Bridge. Equestrian group

and construction began in 1818. Montferrand was a gifted designer, but he had no building experience at all, and made several serious technical mistakes in his project. Soon after construction began, work was suspended, and a special commission had to be set up by the Academy of Arts to make the necessary corrections. The commission was headed by the president of the Academy A. N. Olenin, and among its members there were V. P. Stasov, A. I. Melnikov, A. A. Mikhailov and other eminent architects. It was only with the help of this commission that Montferrand managed to bring the construction to its happy conclusion. Prominent painters K. P. Bryullov and F. A. Bruni, sculptors P. K. Klodt, I. P. Vitali and A. V. Loganovsky, and the best decorators were invited to do the interior.

The cathedral took forty years to build (1818—1858), with the efforts of hundreds of thousands of people. The following facts and figures will give some idea of the scale of this project. This being a swampy site, about 24,000 piles had to be driven in for the foundation, which 11,000 serfs took a year to do, toiling day and night, winter and summer. Each of the 112 columns surrounding the cathedral is a granite monolith. The columns of the lower porticoes are 17 metres high and each one weighs 114 tons. They had to be hewn out of the cliff, transported to St. Petersburg from the quarry near Vyborg, shaped, polished and installed. The columns surrounding the dome-drum are 3 metres shorter than the ones below, but then they had to be hoisted up to that great height.

Many new technical devices were used for the first time, and various innovations were introduced. One of these, was the galvano-plastic method of bronze casting, invented by the Russian scientist Academician Yakobi. In the main, however, all the jobs were done by hand, serf labour being employed as the chief "mechanism".

The tsarist government spared neither human effort nor money for the erection of this gigantic cathedral. The gold-plating took about 25 poods of solid gold and the whole structure cost 23,000,000 rubles—a fabulous sum for that time. Some of the jobs were extremely harmful; thus, many work-

Narva Gate

Moscow Gate

Kamenno-ostrovsky Theatre

men were poisoned and died from the mercury fumes when gold-plating the main dome.

Today, St. Isaac's Cathedral is a museum where the documents and materials on its construction and its architecture have been collected. An excellent view of Leningrad and its suburbs can be had from the top gallery which is 101.5 metres high.

St. Isaac's Square was shaped much later than the city's other important squares, and most of the buildings here date from mid-nineteenth century onward. The oldest is the modestly decorated Myatlev house on the corner of Pochtamtskaya Street (now Soyus Svyazi Street) built in the seventeen-sixties. There is also a house built by Montferrand in 1817—1820 for Lobanov-Rostovsky.

At the far end of the square, behind the Siny (Blue) Bridge, stands the Mariinsky Palace built in 1839—1844 by architect A. I. Stackenschneider. Its elaborate façade is adorned with decorative columns, pilasters and a massive attic. The interior is as resplendent with gilt, decorative moulding, wall and ceiling paintings, and marble. The overuse of ornaments is rather obvious both inside and outside.

The building now houses the Executive Committee of the Leningrad City Soviet and on its façade, under the national emblem of the Russian Federation, are models of the Gold Star, the Orders conferred on the city, and the medal "For the Defence of Leningrad."

Nearer the cathedral, and framing the square on two sides are two similar buildings designed by N. Y. Yefimov, and put up in 1844—1853, for the Departments (Ministries) of Agriculture and State Property. Both these buildings are now used by the research institutes of the Lenin Academy of Agricultural Science of the USSR.

An equestrian monument to Nicholas I was erected in the centre of the square in 1859. The idea of the statue belongs to Montferrand, and it was superbly executed by Klodt. One involuntarily wants to compare it to the Bronze Horseman: the two monuments stand in adjoining squares, both

St. Isaac's Cathedral

The dome of St. Isaac's Cathedral

are equestrian and both face the same way. But here the resemblance ends. Nicholas I, depicted by the sculptor as a lean, uniformed man with a cold, aloof expression, has nothing in common with Peter the Great. Even his horse, as though prancing before the regiments lined up for review, bears no resemblance to Peter's horse which has impetuously leapt to the top of a rock. The pedestals are entirely different too. The "thunder-stone" is a monolith, and it enhances the impression of might, produced by the Bronze Horseman. The other pedestal is completely stultified by the excessive use of every variety of ornament: allegorical figures of Justice, Faith, Wisdom and Might, haut reliefs depicting episodes from the reign of Nicholas I, decorative armour, monograms with crowns, etc.

It is not surprising, therefore, that in expressiveness and impact this monument is considered inferior to Klodt's other works. Being a truthful artist he could hardly be inspired by the image of the gendarme-tsar, and so he was forced to resort to purely outward effects in order to carry out the official order. Hence, the lack of monumentality, the shallowness and the decorativeness. Still, the work itself was executed so artistically and with such technical skill—the statue, it must be remembered, has only two points of support (the horse's hind legs)—that the monument was naturally preserved as an example of the gifted sculptor's work.

The early-twentieth century building of the Hotel Astoria completes St. Isaac's Square.

Former Lobanov-Rostovsky Mansion   Porch of the Lobanov-Rostovsky Mansion

The Executive Committee of the Leningrad City
Soviet (formerly Mariinsky Palace)

Monument to Nicholas I

Astoria Hotel

All-Union Institute of Plant-Breeding

Museum of the Great October Socialist Revolution

The second half of the 19th century and the first decade of the 20th—the period marked by a vigorous development of capitalism in Russia—produced few architectural masterpieces. There was a decline in both architecture and monumental sculpture.

A great number of private-owned buildings were erected in different parts of St. Petersburg in those years, but the architects, pandering to the tastes of their clients, very often went to the extremes of ornateness, over-burdening the façades with a variety of decorative details, or else tried to be extravagantly original. Clashing styles were frequently used in the same building, and when seen next to the perfect creations of the great masters the sight was all the more offensive. The overuse of ornaments and a marked concern with trivia were present even in the works of the more outstanding architects: in the Nikolayevsky Palace (now the Palace of Labour), in the Novo-Mikhailovsky Palace (now the Research Institutes of the USSR Academy of Sciences) built by A. I. Stackenschneider, in the sumptuous palace built in 1873 by A. I. Rezanov for the Grand Duke Vladimir (now the House of Scientists), and in many other large buildings.

Suvorov Museum

Features reminiscent of ancient Russian churches and boyar mansions can also be discerned in some of the buildings of that period. Elements of such stylisation are noticeable in the Suvorov Museum (41, Saltykov-Shchedrin Street), in the Kirov Officers' Club (20, Liteiny Prospekt), and an even more striking example is the church built by A. A. Parland in 1882—1907 on the bank of the Yekaterininsky Canal, the spot where Alexander II was assassinated by members of Narodnaya Volya in 1881. The church was meant to resemble the Cathedral of St. Basil in Moscow, but instead of this remarkable monument of Russian architecture, we have before us a cumbersome, massive construction, unconnected in any way with its environment. The brilliance of the colours and the excessively ornate facing merely stress the impression of disproportion and garishness.

The appearance of the city suffered the most harm from the apartment houses which sprang up with amazing persistence and speed. The owners of these houses naturally cared nothing about city planning, architectural ensembles or national traditions in art. Since the cost of land, in the centre of St. Petersburg especially, kept going up, architects were compelled to build these houses close together, and as a result the streets were turned into long, gloomy corridors lined with featureless, uniform façades. The tiny courts between the houses were like deep wells, without air or light.

The period of the city's capitalist development affected the historical architectural ensembles as well. The numerous banks and shops built mainly in the central streets were designed without any regard for their location or environment. Cases where the design of great architects were barbarously distorted have been mentioned earlier, and more instances can be cited.

The ensemble in Nevsky Prospekt was ruined by the erection of a pretentious building for the Singer Sewing Machine Company (now Book House) by architect P. Y. Suzor, and another one for the Yeliseyev Trading House (now Gastronom No. 1 and the Theatre of Comedy) by architect G. V. Baranovsky. New building materials, metal, and different kinds of stone were freely used in the facing and decoration of these buildings, and their extra-

View of Griboyedov Canal

Church on the bank of Griboyedov Canal

Book House

Theatre of Comedy, and Delicatessen

Kirov Theatre of Opera and Ballet

Monument to Rimsky-Korsakov

Monument to Glinka

vagant architecture clashed with the general appearance of the Nevsky. This was all the more conspicuous because one of these buildings stands opposite the Kazan Cathedral, and the other faces the Pushkin Theatre. The house on the corner of Gogol Street (formerly a bank) hardly belongs here either.

The squares and streets which took shape in the latter half of the nine-teenth century make no claim to artistic harmony and will bear no comparison to the ensembles created at the beginning of that century. A good example is Theatre Square. In the 18th century it was called Carrousel Square. Outdoor fêtes and shows were arranged here for the "common people", and there were merry-go-rounds, booths and stages set up round the square, which took its present name "Theatre Square" from the Bolshoi Kamenny (Stone) Theatre built here in the seventeen-eighties. The theatre has not survived, and in its place we find the somewhat cumbersome and gloomy building of the Conservatoire, erected by V. Nicolas at the end of the 19th century.

In 1859—1860, A. C. Cavos built the Mariinsky Theatre of Opera and Ballet—the largest one in the city—on the other side of the square, in place of the circus which had been destroyed in a fire. Soon after the building was finished, alterations were made to the façade by architect V. A. Schreter. Its extravagance and the tasteless clutter of ornate details deprived it of both monumentality and personality. The opera hall, on the other hand, is very impressive with its upholstery of pale-blue plush and the gilt ornament of the balconies.

The theatre was opened on October 2, 1860, and to this day remains one of the leading musical theatres in the country. Outstanding Russian singers and prima ballerinas have performed on its stage: Chaliapin, Sobinov, Yershov, Preobrazhenskaya, Anna Pavlova, Karsavina, Galina Ulanova, Dudinskaya, and many, many others. The Order of Lenin has been conferred the company on this theatre which is known and acclaimed everywhere in the world as the Kirov Theatre of Opera and Ballet.

This square, which is closely bound up with the history of Russian music,

Health Home on Kamenny Island (former Polovtsev Mansion)

Museum of the Great October Socialist Revolution (former Kshesinskaya's Mansion)

is adorned with monuments to two great Russian composers. One of them is a monument to Glinka (sculptor R. R. Bakh), erected in 1906. The sculptor has portrayed Glinka as a morose, troubled man, and everything about him is commonplace and prosaic. The inspiration, energy and passion of a great composer are completely missing.

The other monument—to Rimsky-Korsakov—was unveiled in November 1952. The sculptors—V. Y. Bogolyubov and V. I. Ingal, both of Leningrad —set themselves the ambitious task of portraying the composer in a moment of inspiration. In their first variant, Rimsky-Korsakov was to be shown standing, to correspond to the Glinka monument. But in the process of work, they renounced this idea and in the final variant the figure is seated. Rimsky-Korsakov is holding a score on his knees, he seems to be running through it and beating time with his right hand. The absorbed expression on his face, the energetic gesture and the easy, habitual posture, convey both the inspired engrossment of the artist and the perseverance of the hard worker.

Inspite of the general decline of architecture at the end of the 19th and the beginning of the 20th centuries, in single instances attempts were made to continue the traditions of Russian classicism. Such, for example, is the Polovtsev Mansion (now a health home) on Kamenny Island, built by A. I. Fomin; such are the houses designed by V. A. Shcuko, A. Y. Belogrud, L. N. Benoit and other major architects. Many of these houses have survived. The street running from the banks of the Neva to Kamenny Island is called Kirovsky Prospekt. It is named after Sergei Kirov, an outstanding Party and Government leader who headed the Leningrad Communists, and lived in house No. 26/28 from 1926 to 1934. This street was laid in 1804—1805 to connect the city centre with the estates on Kamenny Island. Architecturally, it became shaped in late 19th-early 20th centuries.

The Prospekt starts from Revolution Square, the city's oldest. One will notice a two-storey mansion at the back of the square, where two streets intersect. Until the Revolution, this mansion (architect A. I. Gogen) belonged to Nicholas II's favourite, the ballerina Matilda Kshesinskaya. After

Monument to the crew of the destroyer *Steregushchy*

Lev Tolstoi Square. House with the turrets

Monument to Przhevalsky

Monument to Admiral Krusenstern

the overthrow of the autocracy, the Bolshevik Party's leading bodies—the Central and Petrograd Committees—worked in this building from March 11 (March 24, New Style) to July 6 (19), 1917. The Central Committee's military organisation, the *Soldatskaya Pravda* editorial office, and the "Pravda" soldiers' club, also had their premises here. When Lenin returned to Russia on April 3, 1917, he came straight to this house from the Finland Station in the armoured car. The workers who escorted the car remained in front of the house until late and would not go away, and Lenin came out on to the small second-floor balcony again and again and hailed them. In the days that followed he spoke from this balcony on several occasions. Mayakovsky called this mansion "Lenin's smithy" where the victory of the October Revolultion was "hammered into shape". The Museum of the Great October Socialist Revolution was opened here in November 1957.

At the top of Kirovsky Prospekt we find one of the best-known monuments in Leningrad. This is the *Steregushchy,* a monument to the sailors of this destroyer (sculptor K. V. Izenberg) erected in 1911 and dedicated to a heroic episode in the Russo-Japanese war of 1904—1905. The *Steregushchy* was damaged in battle, nearly all the crew were killed, and it seemed that the destroyer would fall easy prey to the enemy. But the two surviving members of the crew, preferring death to surrender, decided to scuttle the ship, and go down with it. The sculptor has depicted the dramatic moment of the sailors opening the cocks and water rushing into the hold.

The *Steregushchy* continues the patriotic theme in Russian monumental sculpture, and gives a dramatic rendering of the Russian Navy's heroic traditions. True, the monument gives only a front view, and there is something contrived in the sculptor's striving to cram his composition into the shape of a cross, but it is impressive, nevertheless.

Unlike the Nevsky with its numerous public buildings—theatres, banks, shops and business offices, Kirovsky Prospekt is mainly a residential street. Houses No. 26/28 (architect L. N. Benoit), No. 63 and No. 65 (architect V. A. Shchuko), the "House with the Turrets" in Lev Tolstoi Square (ar-

Stele portraying the *Aurora* in relief

Cruiser *Aurora*

chitect A. Y. Belogrud), stand out from among the other buildings there for their eloquently expressed identity. It is largely owing to the successes of these architects that Kirovsky Prospekt, for all its heterogeneity of styles, may be said to have personality.

Many new works of monumental sculpture appeared in the streets, squares and parks at the end of the 19th and the beginning of the 20th century. They were interesting in subject matter, but most of them had less artistic merit. As a rule, these monuments and busts were built not at state expense but with money raised by the citizens.

The busts of Gogol, Lermontov, Glinka and Przhevalsky in the Admiralty garden, the small monument to Pushkin (sculptor A. M. Opekushin) in Pushkin Street, and the monument to Lermontov (sculptor B. M. Mikeshin) in Lermontov Prospekt, belong to that period. The monument to Admiral I. F. Krusenstern (sculptor I. N. Schreder) erected on Vasilyevsky Island embankment in 1879, is a typical example to illustrate my point. The Admiral stands calmly peering into the distance. His figure is slender and elegant, but it seems insignificant against the river in the background. The monument has all the faults typical for late nineteenth-early 20th century urban sculpture, the major ones being a lack of monumentality and a penchant for superficial details.

While the majority of the buildings put up in those years were not designed on a very high artistic level, some of them were interesting from the technical point of view. Capitalistic development of industry and transport called for the construction of railway stations, bridges, banks, special schools, etc. Industrial enterprises were opened one after another on the outskirts of the city, and dwellings for the workmen grew up chaotically around them.

The outskirts of St. Petersburg were a horrible sight. The question of planned development did not even arise here. There were rows of wooden shacks, brick barracks, ugly bleak workshops, waste plots, dumps, and mountains of building rubble. The "city fathers" who sat on the City

Duma—rich merchants, factory owners and civil servants—were not going to worry their heads about the outskirts. Many large industrial districts which ought to have been included in the precincts of the city were left out intentionally to save the expense of urbanising them. The allocations for the development of those industrial districts which were officially part of the city were so paltry anyway, that even the barest conveniences could not be provided. A few hundred metres off the centre with its splendid streets and squares lay an entirely different world. A world of hovels and slums, with no electricity, no running water, no sewerage, no paved streets. It was unbelievable that this was a part of that same city which amazed the visitor with the majestic beauty of its granite embankments, great squares and palaces.

Such duality is a characteristic feature of any capitalist town, and St. Petersburg was no exception. Living conditions on the outskirts grew from bad to worse as the city expanded and the population increased. The overwhelming majority of the industrial workers rented beds or a room corner, and only a few were able to afford the luxury of a room to themselves.

This, of course, is no place to look for pre-revolutionary architectural monuments, but then practically every enterprise here, every street and side-street, is a historical monument, the site of glorious revolutionary battles fought by the proletariat of St. Petersburg.

Take the many-kilometre-long Obukhovskaya Oborona Prospekt (formerly Nevskaya Zastava) lined with factories and plants. In the eighteen-nineties Lenin instructed Marxist circles here; in 1901, workers put up a heroic resistance to tsarist troops and the police; strike struggle was waged here by the workers of Semyannikovsky Plant (now Lenin Plant), of Thornton's Cloth Factory (now the Ernst Thälmann Combine), of the Maxwell Factory (now Rabochy Factory), and many other plants.

Industrial enterprises whose workers had taken part in revolutionary battles can be found in every district of Leningrad. The famous Putilov (now Kirov) Works beyond Narvskaya Zastava, the Reschke (now Yegorov)

Factory beyond Moskovskaya Zastava, and many other plants produced thousands of staunch, courageous fighters for the revolutionary army of the working class.

By the turn of the century, St. Petersburg—renamed Petrograd in 1914—became the major centre of the country's revolutionary movement. Petrograd proletarians were in the vanguard during the revolutionary battles of October 1917 when the insurgent people, guided by the Communist Party, won its historical victory. The decree of the Second Congress of Soviets on changing the city's name from Petrograd to Leningrad said: "The workers of Petrograd in their hundreds of thousands were the first to follow Comrade Lenin into fire, and formed the first iron-strong units of the army with which Vladimir Ilyich Lenin defeated the bourgeoisie."

The memorial plaques on a great number of houses in practically every part of the city are reminders of those historic days when the Communist Party was preparing to accomplish the Great October Socialist Revolution.

A stele of pink stone, with the silhouette of *Aurora* carved on it in relief, has been installed opposite the spot from where this cruiser fired the signal for the attack on the evening of October 25, 1917. The stone stands on Krasny Flot (Red Navy) Embankment, beyond the Lt. Schmidt Bridge, opposite the old mansion which houses the Museum of the History of Leningrad. The *Aurora* is moored at a permanent berth of Bolshaya Nevka near the Nakhimov Naval College, a little further upstream. A branch of the Central Naval Museum has been opened in the cruiser.

Their original appearance has been restored to the Lenin house-museum at: apt. 13, 7/4, Pereulok Ilyicha (formerly Bolshoi Kazachy Pereulok), apt. 24, 52/9, Lenin Street (formerly 48/9, Shirokaya Street), apt. 20, 17a, 10th Sovietskaya (formerly 10th Rozhdestvenskaya Street), apt. 20, 1, Serdobolskaya Street, apt. 31, 32, Karpovka Embankment, and apt. 9, 5/7, Khersonskaya Street. The expositions mounted here by the Leningrad Branch of the Lenin Museum deal with the main periods in the Communist Party's struggle for the victory of the Revolution.

Monument to Lenin in front of Finland Station

The whole country has become transformed since the Revolution. Towns and villages have become quite unrecognizable and Leningrad, too, has taken on a new look.

In December 1917, a month after the accomplishment of the Revolution, private-owned houses were municipalised and special house committees were set up to manage them. Thousands of workers who lived in hovels with their families were given the apartments until then occupied by the bourgeoisie; Party and Soviet organisations, childrens' homes and schools and various educational establishments moved into the former palaces, mansions and country estates.

The problems of urban development which arose after 1917 were extremely complex. Old Petrograd with its monstrous social contrasts had to become a new, socialist town where the needs and convenience of the citizens came first. Spacious, light and comfortable dwellings had to be built. At the same time, the architectural monuments and ensembles created by the great masters of the past had to be restored to their original state and kept in good repair.

In the first years following the Revolution, restoration and reconstruction work was mainly done on separate squares and streets (the Field of Mars and the square in front of Smolny, to give just two examples), but beginning from the middle of the nineteen-twenties more ambitious tasks were tackled. The construction of dwelling houses was launched on a large scale, primarily on the outskirts of the city beyond the Narvskaya, Moskovskaya and Nevskaya Zastavas, on Vyborg Side, and in other industrial districts. New streets of modern apartment houses for the workers appeared in place of the wooden shacks inherited from the tsarist days.

The first-born were the Traktornaya and Turbinnaya Streets beyond the former Narvskaya Zastava. The streets were lined with three and four-storey houses spaced at a distance from one another and joined by semi-arches to form an architectural ensemble.

The very fact that the state was building modern dwellings for the working people in place of their old slums had a tremendous social significance. The new houses provided comfortable flats for thousands of working families who, before the Revolution, could never have even dreamed of living in such luxury. Already these first two streets showed how vastly different these industrial districts were going to be from the pre-revolutionary outskirts.

Besides dwelling houses, there had to be shops, tram or bus lines connecting these outlying neighbourhoods with the centre, children's parks, and other amenities. For greater efficiency and speed the outskirts were urbanised in neighbourhoods according to the complex-project method which included the construction of dwelling houses and other premises, the laying of streets and tram lines, the planting of gardens, etc.

In implementation of the decree issued in April 1918 and endorsed by Lenin: "On the removal of monuments erected in honour of tsars and their servants, and on drafting designs of monuments of the Russian Socialist Revolution", a number of monuments which had no artistic or historical value were removed from the streets of Petrograd and Moscow, and work began on the sculptural portrayal of prominent revolutionary figures.

In the middle of the nineteen-twenties, Soviet sculptors produced their first statues of Lenin. The monuments to Lenin in the square in front of the

Finland Station (sculptor S. A. Yevseyev, architects V. A. Shchuko and V. G. Gelfreikh), and in front of Smolny (described earlier) belong to the masterpieces of Soviet monumental sculpture.

Lenin returned to Russia on April 3, 1917, and hundreds of workers, soldiers and sailors came to the Finland Station to meet his train. The telegram giving the time of his arrival was received only that same day, and although it was not a working day the Central Committee managed to let the workers know he was coming. By 10 p.m. the square in front of the railway station was crowded. There were men and women workers from different factories and plants, representatives of the armed forces, and a squad of Baltic sailors who had no little difficulty making their way to the city from Kronstadt; there were armoured cars from the armoured-car division, and also present was the searchlight company from the Peter and Paul Fortress. The square was brightly illumined by the searchlights. The workers carried torches and banners inscribed with words of welcome to Lenin. The train pulled in at 11.10 p.m. Lenin, who was in the fifth car, appeared at the top of the coach steps. The Baltic sailors presented arms, the orchestra played the *Marseillaise,* and the people gathered on the platform gave rousing shouts of welcome. The workers carried Lenin to the station building, and when he reappeared, hailed by a thunderous "Hurrah!", he was lifted on to the armoured car parked in front of the building. Standing on this steel platform, with the searchlights beamed on him, Lenin greeted the people, and this is the moment depicted by sculptor S. A. Yevseyev. Lenin seems to be emphasising his inspired words with his energetic gesture which calls people to struggle and at the same time expresses confidence in the ultimate victory of this struggle.

The composition of the monument is rather unusual: the turret on which the figure stands is moulded into the pedestal comprised of several stacked granite blocks. Structurally, the figure and the pedestal are shifted from the vertical axis, but this unusual device enhances the dynamism of the whole skilfully executed composition.

The monument was unveiled in 1926, on the 9th anniversary of the Revolution, and initially it stood right in front of the station building, on the very spot where Lenin made his speech. Later, when the territory adjoining the

Lenin Square

Monument to Plekhanov

station was reconstructed, the monument was moved to the middle of the newly-formed square where a garden had been laid out. New and newly reconstructed houses rise on two sides of the square, which bears Lenin's name, and the background for the monument which now faces the Neva is provided by the new station building (architects N. V. Baranov, Y. N. Lukin, and P. A. Ashastin). Its glass clock tower is crowned with a thirty-metre high spire made from stainless steel. The passenger hall, with a 35-square-metre ceiling, is so enormous that no matter how large the crowd of incoming or outgoing passengers it always seems roomy and spacious.

Among the other monuments erected in the nineteen-twenties and thirties, we might mention the monument to G. V. Plekhanov in front of the Technological Institute (sculptor I. Y. Gintsburg, 1925) the monument to V. Volodarsky in Nevsky district (sculptor M. G. Manizer, 1925), and the memorial to the victims of Bloody Sunday—January 9, 1905, in Preobrazhensky Cemetery (also by M. G. Manizer, 1931).

The monument to G. V. Plekhanov is not a great success. It looks too small and insignificant in comparison to the surrounding buildings, and the impression is further spoilt by the strangely disproportionate figures of Plekhanov and the worker with a banner on the pedestal.

The works of M. G. Manizer are much more interesting. He placed his monument to Volodarsky on the Neva embankment, close to the spot where this outstanding revolutionary was murdered by the Social-Revolutionaries in 1918. Manizer has depicted him at the conclusion of the speech he has just made: he seems about to step down from the speaker's platform, the excitement has not yet cooled on his face, and his right arm is flung upward in an expressive gesture. Volodarsky is shown wearing ordinary workday clothes, his overcoat is carelessly slipping down from one shoulder, but there is nothing prosaic about him. This monument is best viewed from the Neva.

The memorial to the victims of Bloody Sunday is a majestic composition, intended to be seen from afar. A gigantic figure of a workman is mounted on a tall pedestal. In one hand he is holding an urn, and his other arm is raised as though calling people forward to avenge this innocently shed blood. The events of January 9 are shown in haut relief on the pedestal. What Manizer wanted to render was how the mentality of the masses changed in that single day. The first three figures are bringing the petition; the ones coming behind them are being shot down; and the last ones are already the insurgent people.

The monument was unveiled in 1931, on the 26th anniversary of Bloody Sunday. Thousands of Leningraders come here on commemoration day every year to pay a tribute to these victims of tsarism.

From the middle of the nineteen-twenties the erection of new apartment houses and public buildings, many of which formed the pivots of new squares and architectural ensembles, assumed a larger scale with every year. They were designed by Leningrad's leading architects A. S. Nikolsky, A. I. Gegello, D. L. Krichevsky, Y. A. Levinson, I. I. Fomin, N. A. Trotsky and others.

Two large houses of culture were opened in 1927, on the 10th anniversary of Soviet power: the Gorky House of Culture at the Narva Gates (architects A. I. Gegello and D. L. Krichevsky), and the Vyborg House of Culture, reconstructed from an old house by the same architects. These two structures were of a style unknown in pre-revolutionary Russia. The Gorky House of Culture deserves especial attention. The massive dark-grey building faces the busy Stachki Square in front of the Narva Gates. The glass façade is divided by three-edged pilaster strips, and the air of monumentality is further enhanced by the two imposing risalitos to the right and left of the glass front.

This is a historical site. There was a school here before, where in August 1917 the Sixth Congress of the Communist Party set the Party and the people on the road to an armed uprising. This fact is recorded in the memorial plaque near the front entrance. There is another memorial board on which the words of Gorky, spoken after a visit to this house of culture, are inscribed: "I wish these centres of culture great strength, the strength of fire that turns iron ore into steel. Just as the hands of workers make needles, nibs for the writers, chisels and the most complex machines from a mass of steel, so must the working class create masters of art and culture from its own midst."

There is a concert hall, seating more than two thousand people, a smaller cinema hall, several lecture halls, lounges, and rooms for various hobby

Monument to Volodarsky

Monument to the victims of January 9, 1905

Gorky House of Culture   Kirov House of Culture

Komsomol Square

circles. Thousands of people spend their evenings here: they come to see a film, a show, play a game of chess, browse through the newspapers and magazines, or work on their particular hobby.

The concert hall has no balconies, which were inevitable in the old theatres, and only the dress circle going up at a slope to the back of the hall, and boxes on the sides. This arrangement made for excellent visibility, and the idea was copied in many other concert halls.

The Lenin House of Culture (architect V. A. Shchuko) and the Textile Workers' House of Culture (architict S. O. Ovsyannikov) were built soon afterwards behind the Nevskaya Zastava. Architects Y. A. Levinson and V. O. Munts built the Lensoviet Palace of Culture on Petrograd Storona, and architects N. A. Trotsky and S. N. Kazak—the Kirov House of Culture on Vasilyevsky Island. Actually, there were several houses of culture opened in each one of Leningrad's industrial districts.

Monument to Komsomol

The improvement and reconstruction of city streets and squares continued in the late nineteen-twenties. Turgenev (formerly Pokrovskaya) Square was planted with trees and given a new look; the Bolshoi Prospekt on Vasilyevsky Island was widened; the Strelka of Yelagin Island—a very popular place for walks—had a granite parapet with stone lions put in by architect L. A. Ilyin in 1926; and improvements were made to Labour (formerly Blagoveshchenskaya) Square, Ligovsky Prospekt, and many other principal throughfares.

The early nineteen-thirties marked a vigorous upsurge in urban development. The decisions of the June Plenary Session of the Central Committee of the CPSU on the development of housing in Moscow and the USSR in general, and the appeal of the Council of People's Commissars of the USSR and the Central Committee of the Party about the development of Leningrad, were published in 1931, opening new prospects for the city.

It is difficult to describe even briefly all that was achieved in the ten years from 1931 to 1941. Apartment houses, clubs, schools, hospitals, cinemas, stadiums and administrative buildings, erected in that decade, can be found in Vyborg Storona, beyond the Narvskaya, Moskovskaya and Nevskaya Zastavas, and on the Malaya Okhta. The central streets were renovated, new embankments and bridges were built, parks and gardens were laid out—in short, the city became more and more beautiful with every day. Sergei Kirov, who headed the Leningrad Party organisation and directed the city's development with exemplary enthusiasm, used to say that Leningrad had all the makings of a truly socialist city, of a city truly worthy of the name it bears.

In 1935, the Central Committee adopted the decision to draw up a general plan of Leningrad's development, with priority given to the Kirovsky, Moskovsky and Nevsky districts—southern districts which were safe from inundation even in the worst floods and which had many vacant plots suitable for construction. Many of the existing buildings here, especially on the main throughfares—Stachki Prospekt, Moskovsky Prospekt and Obukhovskaya Oborona Prospekt—were put up in the late nineteen-thirties in implementation of the above-mentioned plan.

One of them is the apartment house, whose address is 79, Moskovsky

Nevsky District. Ivanovskaya Street

Prospekt, designed by L. A. Ilyin who was then the city's chief architect and who died in besieged Leningrad during the war. Construction of this building on the site of the city dump began in 1938, and only the two wings were finished by 1941 when the war began. The whole was completed in 1951, strictly according to Ilyin's design. The main façade is set back from the street, and its pale-coloured walls make a very pleasing background for the green lawns of the garden in front of it. The strict logic of its design, the well-balanced proportions of the different components, and the good colour scheme, make it a most attractive building.

Comparing it with the pre-revolutionary apartment houses, we shall see how the very principles of designing had changed. In the past, the architect building a house on a piece of private-owned land, had to make the utmost use of it and therefore the spaces between the houses were reduced to a minimum, depriving most of the flats of light and air. In Ilyin's design, and in the other post-revolutionary apartment houses, we observe emphasis on good lighting throughout, for the ground floors as well. The buildings are spaced far apart, and nothing interferes with the access of light to all the rooms. There are no well-like courts, no gloomy corridors of streets, no congestion, and consequently conditions in these districts are immeasurably healthier than before.

Speaking of administrative buildings erected in those years, mention must be made of the one built by N. A. Trotsky at the further end of Moskovsky Prospekt, not far from the city's southern boundary. At the time there were hardly any large buildings nearby, and the sight of this great, tall house with its endless rows of windows, palatial façade and sculptural decorations, seemed very strange in the middle of the wasteland. This waste has been built up in recent years, and still Trotsky's building looks as imposing as ever among them, and actually dominates the square in front of it.

The long façade is set back from the street to a distance of some 200 metres, and it looks both impressive and slightly severe, especially the central part which is decorated with semi-columns. From the ground to the tip of the emblem of the Russian Federation on its roof, this part of the building is approximately 50 metres high. The semi-columns support a broad sculptured frieze whose theme is the peaceful labour of Soviet people.

The building was to have a large conference hall, more than 500 offices and other premises, but work on the interior was suspended owing to the outbreak of the war. Being close to the front line, the building suffered grave damage from enemy bombs and shells. However, it has now been fully restored.

Other houses which attract notice in Moskovsky Prospekt include the somewhat ornately cumbersome Soyuzpushnina House where international fur auctions are held every year (architect D. F. Friedman, 1938); the originally designed building of the District Soviet (architects I. I. Fomin and V. G. Daugul, 1935); and school No. 370 built by architect S. V. Vasilkovsky from prefabricated blocks which, at the time, was an advance in building technology.

Needless to say, the above examples hardly do justice to what was done in the late nineteen-thirties for the development of the southern districts. Mention should also be made of the Nevsky District Soviet (architects

Monument to Kirov in Kirov Square

Kirov Square

Lenin Komsomol Theatre

Y. A. Levinson and I. I. Fomin), of the new buildings that completely transformed the old Shchemilovka in Nevsky district, and the apartment houses in Stachki Prospekt.

The monument to Sergei Kirov (sculptor N. V. Tomsky, architect N. A. Trotsky) in the square in front of the Kirovsky District Soviet was unveiled in 1938. This admirable work of monumental sculpture is one of Leningrad's adornments.

The memory of Sergei Kirov is especially revered by the inhabitants of Leningrad where this outstanding Communist worked for many years, especially distinguishing himself in the field of urban improvement. The district which bears his name is the old Narvskaya Zastava, transformed in the years of Soviet power.

N. V. Tomsky produced an inspired piece of work: in his statue, Kirov is a great citizen, and at the same time a kind-hearted, simple person. He seems to be walking with an energetic stride against the wind which blows back the skirts of his coat. In his left hand he has a copy of *Pravda,* and with the sweeping gesture of his right hand he seems to be inviting everybody to take a look all round, at the transformed district. Kirov wears his charming smile, remembered well by anyone who had ever seen him. The tetrahedral pedestal made of grey-green polished Karelian granite is adorned with bronze plaques embossed with scenes from Soviet history. "Civil War", "Socialist Emulation", "Bright Road" make the themes of these many-figure compositions.

Erected in the middle of a large square, the monument is seen well from every side. A new apartment house was built here after the war, and its façade serves as a background for it from the side of Stachki Square. The garden was laid out in 1954.

While in the nineteen-thirties construction mainly went on the outskirts, some important buildings were put up in the centre as well. One of them is the Lenin Komsomol Theatre built in 1933—1939 in Lenin Park, Petrogradskaya Storona, next to the old Narodny Dom (People's House). The architects, N. A. Miturich and V. P. Makashev, wanted to introduce some novel features into the conventional theatre-house architecture. There are no narrow little passages, small foyers and tiny dressing rooms, generally

Heroes Avenue in Moskovsky Victory Park

found in the old theatres. One enters a spacious vestibule from which a wide flight of stairs leads to a large foyer. The hall, which seats more than 1,500 people, has only the pit and the dress circle, and is so cleverly designed that a view of the stage is never blocked wherever one sits. Rehearsing rooms, dressing rooms, sewing rooms, and other workrooms, take up a good half of the building.

The main façade is quite majestic. The tall entrance, decorated with Corinthian columns supporting a semi-circular niche containing a model of the state emblem of the USSR looks most effective against the park background.

The building was badly damaged during the siege of Leningrad, but by 1947 it had been fully restored.

Although a great amount of work had already been done, the further development of Leningrad was arrested by Hitler Germany's perfidious attack on the USSR. In 1941 a new stage began for the city—a time of grim trials and struggle.

The countenance of the city changed. Leningrad became part of the front line. The seventh tram stop from the Kirov Works was the first line of defence.

For nine hundred days—from September 1941 to January 1944—Leningrad was in the vice of an enemy blockade. But the city with a population of several million people withstood the siege, and emerged victorious from the battle—a feat unprecedented in history. The nazis dropped thousands of bombs on the streets of Leningrad. Bombs and shells hit the Admiralty, the Winter Palace, the Engineers' Castle and other precious edifices.

That first winter was the worst: there was no fuel, no electricity, no trams, no buses, no running water, and no food. Hunger mowed people down ruthlessly. It seemed impossible to live in this city, and the nazi newspapers predicted the imminent fall of Leningrad, strangled by the blockade, and actually named the day and the hour when Hitler's armies would goosestep along the Neva embankments. The streets were mostly deserted that first grim winter; fires from the incendiary bombs kept reaking out, the demolition bombs blasted many-storey buildings, shell fragments screamed as they hit the pavements, and the city appeared dead.

Alexander Matrosov. Moskovsky Victory Park.

But Leningrad was alive, it was alive, it was fighting, and its defenders stood to the death.

A "road of life", as it was called, was laid across the ice of Lake Ladoga, and lorries loaded with provisions, armaments, ammunition and fuel made their way to Leningrad in a steady stream. Planes landed on the snow-drifted airstrips. The whole country was sending aid to the besieged city. Leningrad factories worked round the clock, manufacturing armaments for the front, for victory; Leningrad's scientists continued their research work; Leningrad's architects, sculptors and builders who rescued and kept safe the city's art treasures were already then planning the construction projects that would be launched after the war.

The immediate task confronting the architects of Leningrad was to save the masterpieces of architecture and sculpture. Lenin's monument in front of Finland Station and the Bronze Horseman were protected with sandbags and a thick layer of earth; Klodt's horses were taken down from Anichkov Bridge; the Admiralty spire was draped in special protective cases; the gold of the Peter and Paul spire and the dome of St. Isaac's Cathedral was painted for camouflage; a camouflage net was stretched over the Smolny, and the façades of the principal buildings merged with the surrounding landscape. These efforts were not wasted, and practically all the unique works of art were preserved.

Leningrad covered itself with new glory in the war years. In January 1945, at a big meeting held at the Kirov Theatre—the serious damage done to which had already been repaired—Mikhail Kalinin presented Leningrad with the Order of Lenin for valour in battle with the enemy and said that what the Leningraders had done would be remembered forever, by all the generations to come.

The Gold Star was also awarded to Leningrad, a hero-city, in 1965 on the 20th anniversary of victory.

Leningrad welcomed Victory Day with the wounds still fresh, but it was as dignified and beautiful as ever. Restoration work had begun a year earlier, in January 1944, as soon as the salute was fired to announce that the enemy storming it had been routed and the siege lifted. People old and young—pensioners, housewives, office workers and school children—in short, all

Yelagin Island. View of the former Yelagin Palace

the inhabitants of Leningrad—joined forces in the repair work, toiling in the sweat of their brow to make their city more beautiful and splendid than ever.

The damage was heavy indeed. Houses totalling three million square metres of dwelling space had been destroyed, houses with a total of two million square metres of dwelling space had been damaged, the communal services and city transport were in a bad state, a great number of the wooden structures on the outskirts and the nearest suburbs had been taken apart for fuel, and practically all the remaining dwelling houses were in need of repairs.

Restoration work and the quickest construction of dwellings naturally came first. But already in those first post-war years, as the main work progressed, new architectural ensembles were shaped and new monuments appeared.

Two new Victory parks were started that first post-war autumn of 1945. It is an ancient tradition to celebrate the victory of Russian arms by planting gardens and parks. And true to this tradition, the inhabitants turned out in their thousands on October 7, 1945, to plant a tree in the new parks, considering it an honour and a pleasant duty.

The Moskovsky district's Victory Park is situated in the southern part of town, on the site of Syzran Field—a large waste plot which, in pre-revolutionary times, it would never have occurred to anybody to make into a spot of green so essential for this factory district. The park (area 68 hectares) was designed by architects Y. I. Katonin and V. D. Kirkhoglani. There is a clear-cut pattern of straight walks and neatly trimmed trees, and there are also lots of picturesque spots of "wild" nature. People enjoy leafing through a magazine at one of the open-air reading rooms or play a game of chess in a pleasantly shady pavilion, and many go boating on the numerous small ponds. They make a very pleasant feature, and everyone imagines that they had always been here, which is not so at all. There are no bodies of water in this part of town, and the architects very cleverly created these ponds using the pits made by the nearby brickworks. What is more, at their special request the brickworks made two square pits with small islands left in the middle. The pits were filled with water and canals were built

Kirov Stadium. Square in front of the main ent-   Kirov Stadium
rance

Yubileiny Palace of Sports

Insurrection (Vosstaniye) Square

Kirovsky Prospekt

Monument to Gorky

2, Kirovsky Prospekt

to connect them, making one of the main attractions and adornments of the park.

The statuary is dedicated to the heroic battles of the Great Patriotic War. The Avenue of Heroes—the central walk—starts from the main entrance, adorned with propylaea. At the top of the avenue there is a fountain whose sprays fall in a fanciful basket design. Ranged along the avenue, on left and right, are the busts of Leningraders who were twice awarded the title of Hero of the Soviet Union: pilots V. M. Golubev, V. N. Osipov, Y. P. Fyodorov, V. I. Rakov, N. V. Chelnokov, and Marshal S. I. Bogdanov of the Armoured Forces. In the side avenues there are monuments to Zoya Kosmodemyanskaya (sculptor M. G. Manizer) and Alexander Matrosov (sculptor L. Y. Eidlin). Further on, there is the statue of Raymonde Dien, a courageous French woman (sculptor Ts. Diveyeva).

Monument to Chernyshevsky

The other Victory Park is in the north-west part of the city, on the shore of the Gulf of Finland, and it takes up most of Krestovsky Island. This is one of the three islands called Kirovsky Islands which were developed, with Sergei Kirov's personal participation, into health resorts for all the citizens of Leningrad. The other two are Kamenny Island (now called Ostrov Trudyashchikhsya) which has health and holiday homes, and Yelagin Island, occupied by the Kirov (Central) Recreation Park.

In designing this park, architects A. S. Nikolsky, N. N. Stepanov and others made use of what remained of the old Byeloselsky. The total area exceeds 160 hectares, divided in two by the two-kilometre-long lime avenue which is a continuation of Morskoi Prospekt and leads to the shore, ending at the main entrance to the Kirov Stadium.

This stadium is an inalienable part of Victory Park whose construction began in the early nineteen-thirties. Architect A. S. Nikolsky and his co-authors K. I. Kashin and N. N. Stepanov conceived it as an artificially built hill on the shore of the Gulf with a depression made in the middle where grandstands would be placed around and up the slopes. Powerful dredging machines dug up more than a million cubic metres of earth from the bottom of the Gulf of Finland to erect this hill, and another million-and-a-half cubic metres of sand was used to raise the level of the site. This preliminary work was, in the main, finished by 1941.

Construction was resumed after the war, and the new stadium was opened on July 30, 1950.

At the main entrance stands a bronze monument to Sergei Kirov, designed by sculptor V. B. Pinchuk.

Behind the monument are two symmetrically placed pavilions where out-of-town sportsmen can be accommodated. There are bedrooms, changing rooms, showers, and other service premises in these pavilions which are connected with the playing field by tunnels. Two wide staircases, decorated with sculpture, a fountain and water cascades, lead to the top of the artificial 16-metre high hill. There are similar, though less ornate, staircases going up the other sides as well. A balcony runs round the top of the hill, and looking down from there one will see the floor of this earthen bowl with its green football field, race track, basketball court, volleyball court, high jumps, long jumps, and so forth. Benches are ranged along the inner slopes of the hill, and there is enough room to seat 80,000 people. The total length of these benches, if stretched into a straight line, equals 32 kilometres. There are 52 staircase-aisles running down the slopes between the benches. So much for the seating arrangements, but there is also enough standing room for about 20,000, and the more interesting matches—international metes, all-Union and Leningrad championships—are usually watched by more than 100,000 spectators. Leningraders come here even when there's nothing on, just to relax on the green slopes, enjoying the quiet and the fresh sea air, gazing at the expanse of the Gulf of Finland and watching the white-saled yachts in the distance. This artificial hill is so well integrated into the park that it seems a natural component of the landscape.

The architects who designed the stadium were worried by the thought that there was no proper outlet to the sea within the precincts of the town since the shoreline was built up with factory buildings, warehouses, and

Rossiya Hotel   Moskovsky Prospekt near Victory Square

Ploshchad Lenina (Lenin Square) Metro Station.
Entrance pavilion

Pushkinskaya Metro Station. Entrance pavilion

various structures of a temporary nature. Such was the view of Leningrad from the Gulf. Giving the city a "sea front" was set down as one of the important tasks in the general plan of development. The green slopes of the artificial hill make the beginnings of this "sea front", and as soon as the surrounding territory is re-designed and brought in line with it, the panorama will be complete.

When repairing the war damage, the architects and builders did not simply try to put everything back in place, but took a much more broad-minded approach to their task. New and better buildings were erected in place of some of the bleaker apartment houses, if they were badly damaged. But when it came to the architectural monuments, created by the great masters of the past, these were handled with the greatest care. In many cases whole ensembles were freed from the distortions made in the period of capitalist development and given back their original look. This was done in Arts Square, and the territory in front of the Engineers' Castle. Improvements were made to Nevsky and Kirovsky Prospekts. The tram lines were removed from Nevsky Prospekt in 1950—1951, the street was asphalted, the pavements were made twice as wide, better street lights were installed, and a garden was laid out in Vosstanye (Insurrection) Square in front of Moscow Railway Station. Kirovsky Prospekt was similarly improved, and new houses built on the site of destroyed buildings.

The modern construction of Kirovsky Prospekt begins from Lenin Park at the intersection with Maxim Gorky Prospekt. The five-storey apartment house built on the corner by architects O. I. Guryev and V. M. Fromzel has an attractive pale-coloured façade which rounds the corner in a concave semi-circle and is modestly decorated with pilasters, pretty balconies, rusticated plinth floor, and a graceful balustrade. It holds a most responsible position for it sets the tone, as it were, tor the newly built up part of the Prospekt. A monument to Gorky (by sculptor V. V. Isayeva) was unveiled in front of this house in 1968.

At the intersection with Ulitsa Mira (Peace Street) there is a small square dominated by a building designed by O. I. Guryev and A. P. Shcherbenka, and further on there is another house designed by O. I. Guryev and V. M. Fromzel which makes an integral part of the panorama.

Leningrad Metro Administration

Kirovsky Zavod (Kirov Works) Metro Station. Entrance pavilion

Elektrosila Metro Station. Entrance pavilion

Avtovo Metro Station. Entrance pavilion

Avtovo Metro Station

Dozens of other streets were similarly improved and modernised. Trees have been planted along Chernyshevsky and Zhelyabov streets; the banks of Obvodny Canal, between Baltic Station and Moskovsky Prospekt—the dirtiest and most neglected in the past—have become unrecognisable; waste plots have been transformed into shady gardens.

The development of the outskirts, started way back in the nineteen-twenties, is continuing on an increasing scale. A person who has not been to Leningrad for several years would not recognise the Staraya Derevnya (Old Village) and the Novaya Derevnya (New Village) which now make a picturesque entrance to Leningrad's holiday zone, or Engels Prospekt, or Stachki Prospekt.

Moskovsky Prospekt, one of the city's longest, is growing more handsome with every year. Starting from Peace (Mir) Square in the centre of the city, this ten-kilometre-long street runs south to Victory Square (Ploshchad Pobedy) where it branches into the Moscow and Kiev highways. The Prospekt may be divided into three parts: the first, from Peace Square to the Obvodny Canal, the second from the Canal to the Elektrosila Plant, and the third—from this plant to Victory Square. The first part was built up before the revolution. The prospekt is narrow here, it looks rather glum and cramped between the rows of tall stone buildings lining it. True, some improvements have been made in the course of the city's restoration.

Peace Square bears no resemblance to the Sennaya Square as it was called before, where fodder used to be sold (hence the name, derived from *seno,* meaning hay), and which gradually became cluttered with ugly market stalls and other such structures. The poor of St. Petersburg lived in the dark and squalid apartment houses facing this square, and their wretched existence has been described in the works of many Russian classics. Sennaya Square was also the place where punishment was publicly meted out: serfs found guilty of some offense were beaten here with whips and birch rods.

The square was cleared of market stalls and other such structures in the late nineteen-thirties, and after the war trees were planted round it, the bomb-damaged houses were repaired, and a new building enclosing the square was erected. Further reconstruction is envisaged in the next few years.

Park Pobedy (Victory Park) Metro Station. Entrance pavilion

The intersection of Moskovsky Prospekt and the Fontanka embankment has been embellished with two buildings whose semi-circular façades make room for two small lawns in front of them. Further south, a garden has been laid out between the Technological Institute and the Obvodny Canal on the site of the former Klin market, and fenced in with a wrought-iron grille designed by architects V. A. Kamensky and G. L. Ashrapyan.

Beyond the Obvodny Canal, Moskovsky Prospekt assumes an entirely different character. It widens out to begin with, and is lined with modern buildings—well-spaced apartment houses with lawns between them. The further south one continues the more one is impressed by the scale of construction going on here—there are newly tenanted apartment houses, some nearing completion and others under construction. While the stretch as far as the Elektrosila Plant was built up pre-war in the main, the next stretch is entirely post-war. A new overbridge has been built by architects V. D. Kirkhoglani and G. K. Patrikeyev, and now the whole prospekt, without narrowing down at all, passes comfortably under its 52-metre span.

New squares are gradually taking shape in the new neighbourhoods. One of these is the Chernyshevsky Square opposite Victory Park. A monument to Nikolai Chernyshevsky, an outstanding Russian revolutionary democrat, was unveiled here in 1947. The sculptor, V. V. Lishev, portrayed him as a youthful thinker, engrossed in his dreams of a better future for his country. He is sitting on a bench with an open book in his hands, lost in thought.

At the rear end of the square rises the ten-storey building of the Rossiya Hotel, erected in 1962 by architects B. N. Zhuravlyov, P. A. Areshev and V. E. Struzman. Its main entrance faces the central avenue of Victory Park. This light-coloured, elegantly simple modern building makes a good background for the monument to Chernyshevsky. The hotel is one of the biggest in Leningrad: its 414 rooms can accommodate 612 people at a time.

A new square is taking shape at the end of Moskovsky Prospekt where it branches out into the Moscow and Kiev highways. It has already been named Victory Square (Ploshchad Pobedy), and it is to be the gateway to Leningrad from the direction of Moscow. Two multi-storey buildings will be erected on either side to form a sort of propylaea, giving a panoramic

Theatre for Young Spectators

view of Moskovsky Prospekt. In the centre, it is planned to erect a monument to victory over the enemy in the Great Patriotic War of1941—45.

Twenty years is not a very long stretch of time in the life of a city, but anyone who last saw Leningrad shortly after the war and went there now, would be amazed at the countless new buildings erected in the interim.

Not all of them are equally good, of course. An obvious and unwarranted striving for pomposity mars many of the houses built in the first post-war decade. For example, several apartment houses on Revolution Square, in Stachki Prospekt, Moskovsky Prospekt, and elsewhere are decorated with massive columns, turrets, spires and all kinds of ornamental details. Such decorativeness is entirely foreign to modern architecture, nor is it in keeping with the city's architectural traditions. On the other hand, there are some new streets that completely lack personality.

The Leningrad metro was opened on November 15, 1955, and very soon it became as much a part of the city as, say, the spire of the Admiralty or the Kirov Stadium, and was included, together with a visit to the branch of the Lenin Museum, the Hermitage and the Russian Museum, in all sightseeing tours.

The first Metro lines, stretching for more than 14 kilometres, connected the city's major industrial centres—Vyborg Side and Kirovsky district. The first section of approximately 11 kilometres, from Moscow Railway Station to Avtovo, the south-western extreme, was opened in 1955; by the summer of 1958 the line was extended northward from Moscow Station to Finland Station, passing under the Neva, and from Avtovo further south-west to Dachnoye. Thus, all the five railway stations were connected by Metro lines.

The second line began to function in 1961. It was laid under Moskovsky Prospekt and connected Victory Park with the Technological Institute. In the summer of 1963, the line was extended to Ploshchad Mira (Peace Square), then to Nevsky Prospekt, and thence—passing under the Neva—to Petrograd Side, and Lev Tolstoi Square.

Another line is under construction, connecting Alexander Nevsky Square with Vasilyevsky Island. The first section was set in operation in 1967, on the occasion of the 50th anniversary of Soviet power. In due course it will be extended to the south-eastern extreme of the city—to the Nevsky

Kalinin Square

Monument to Dobrolyubov

District, one of the largest new industrial and residential districts in Leningrad.

There are eleven stations along the first line. All of them are faced with marble and granite, flooded with light and decorated with statuary, relief sculpture, pictures and other ornaments on the theme of the Soviet people's creative endeavour and the important events in the life of the country.

The Ploshchad Lenina (Lenin Square) Station, the point of the Metro train's departure, was designed by architect A. K. Andreyev. One of its vestibules is built into a wing of Finland Station, and the entrance hall is decorated with a large panel in mosaics, by artists A. A. Mylnikov and A. L. Korolev, depicting Lenin's arrival at this station on April 3, 1917. The pylons of the underground hall are faced with Ukrainian red granite and crowned with a polished metal cornice.

Chernyshevskaya Station, faced with pale grey marble, is severely simple. The underground hall was designed by A. V. Zhuk and S. G. Maiofis, and the surface vistibule by A. S. Getskin and V. P. Shuvalova.

The next stop is Ploshchad Vosstanya (Insurrection Square) built by

Monument to Kondratyev

I. I. Fomin, V. V. Gankevich and B. N. Zhuravlyov. There are two entrances: one next to Moscow Station, and the other facing it on Nevsky Prospekt. The events of the Great October Socialist Revolution make the theme of the decoration. The pylons are adorned with bronze medallions, depicting such historical moments as: Lenin making a speech from the top of the armoured car at Finland Station, Lenin in Razliv, the *Aurora* firing its signal, the storming of the Winter Palace, and Lenin proclaiming the establishment of Soviet power at the Second Congress of Soviets.

A few minutes later the train stops at Vladimirskaya Station, which is situated between two busy streets: Vladimirsky and Zagorodny Prospekts. This station, designed by G. I. Alexandrov, A. V. Zhuk and A. I. Pribulsky, is dignified and simple. Its only ornament is a colourful mosaic (entitled "Abundance") on the portal of the escalator hall made at the mosaics workshop of the USSR Academy of Art.

Next, the train comes to Push-kinskaya Station. Its entrance is next door to the Vitebsk Railway Terminus from which, at the week-end, thousands of Leningraders

Monument to the heroes of the Oktyabrsky District Division of People's Volunteers

leave by train for Pushkin (formerly Tsarskoye Selo) to spend their two days-off in this picturesque suburb. The underground hall was designed by L. M. Polyakov and V. A. Petrov, and the surface vestibule by A. A. Grushke, A. S. Getskin and V. P. Shuvalova. The walls and ceilings are decorated with painting. The Pushkin theme makes the leitmotif. At the far end of the underground hall there is a statue of Pushkin (sculptor M. K. Anikushin) with a painting of the Tsarskoye Selo park (artist M. A. Engelke) forming the background.

The three stations Ploshchad Vosstanya, Vladimirskaya and Pushkinskaya have one common feature in their construction: the vaults of the underground halls are supported by massive pylons. Architects A. M. Sokolov and A. K. Andreyev, who designed the Technological Institute Station at the intersection of Moskovsky Prospekt, Zagorodny Prospekt and First Krasnoarmeyskaya Street, used slender columns, faced with white Urals marble, instead of pylons, and as a result the hall seems very spacious and lofty. There are several institutes in this district—the Technological, the Civil Engineers, and others,—and it is not surprising that the leitmotif of the decoration is the development of Russian science. The surface vestibule is built into the house where the Leningrad Metro Administration has its offices. The semi-circular façade of this building is decorated with a massive colonnade above a high plinth floor. This station is one of the busiest since the two lines cross here.

The next, Baltiyskaya (Baltic) Station was designed by M. K. Benoit, A. I. Kubasov and F. F. Oleinik, and the theme of its decoration is the glorious history of the Baltic Navy.

From here the train heads for Kirovsky district, the former Narvskaya Zastava. The first stop is at Narvskaya Station on Stachki Square. It was built by architects A. V. Vasilyev, D. S. Goldgor and S. B. Speransky. "Happiness in Work" is the subject of the interior decoration.

The next stop is at the famous Kirov Works. The Kirovskaya Station was designed by architect A. K. Andreyev. On the surface there is a detached square building surrounded by a graceful colonnade which gives an architectural finishing touch to the intersection of Stachki Prospekt and a side street. The underground hall is decorated with columns crowned with the

Piskarevsky Memorial Cemetery. Figure of Motherland

emblems of the leading branches of industry. A bust of Lenin stands on a tall pedestal at the far end of the hall. The columns are made from wrought-iron tubings—never practised in subway construction before—and faced with silvery grey marble.

The stop after that is Avtovo Station, located not far from where the front line was during the siege of Leningrad. The Soviet tank, mounted on a tall pedestal and flanked by two obelisks, is a memento of those years. The decoration of the station (architects Y. A. Levinson and A. A. Grushke) is dedicated to the heroic defence of Leningrad. The following words are inscribed in letters of gold on the cornice of the entrance hall: "Glory to the valiant defenders of Leningrad, the hero-city!" A composition in relief sculpture with a soldier, sailor and partisan for the central figures decorates one of the walls in the circular hall. After Avtovo the train emerges from the tunnel and continues to Dachnoye across the new residential districts.

The second Metro line has nine stations which look simpler and more severe in design than the underground palaces of the first line. There is less sculpture here, less marble and other expensive facing material, but the underground halls are very attractive just the same. Tiles, aluminium, glass plastics and other modern materials have been used with great success. The highlights of Frunzenskaya, Gorkovskaya and Elektrosila stations are the haut-relief portraits of Frunze and Gorky in the first two respectively, and the decorative panel called "The Electrification of the Country" in the third one.

Petrogradskaya and Victory Park (Park Pobedy) Stations—the first and the last in the second Metro line—are very interesting from the constructional point of view. There are no passenger platforms here, and one steps into the train through one of the glass doors which slide back automatically, to correspond exactly with the opening doors of the train when it comes to a stop.

The surface vestibules of the second Metro line are also smaller and less ornate than those of the first line. Some of them, like Victory Park, Elektrosila, Frunzenskaya and Gorkovskaya stations, are enclosed in small round pavilions, designed by A. S. Getskin and V. P. Shuvalova, but most of them are built into multi-storey houses, and Nevsky Prospekt Station has no

Karl Marx Prospekt

Avtovo. Stachki Prospekt

surface pavilion at all, just an entrance to the underground hall. Before many years have passed dozens of new Metro stations will appear on the map of Leningrad, and the present length of the underground railway will be increased several times over.

In recent years several new architectural ensembles have been completed. One of them is the Komsomol Square ensemble in Kirovsky district. The square is encircled by three large seven-storey buildings, designed by V. A. Kamensky and S. G. Maiofis. In the centre, where a small garden has been laid out, a monument to the Komsomol was unveiled in 1968.

The semi-circular square near the "Svetlana" factory on Engels Prospekt, designed by B. F. Below and L. L. Schreter, is an interesting example of ensemble building.

Another architectural ensemble is taking shape in the centre of the town, close to Vitebsk Railway Station, in the vicinity of the former Semyonovsky parade-ground where executions and public punishments were staged in tsarist times. The pivot of this ensemble is the Theatre for Young Spectators built in 1962 by A. V. Zhuk. This large, cheerful building is attractively laconic in its modern design. The hall, which seats a thousand people, is built as an amphitheatre, and is both comfortable and inviting. The stage has been equipped with the most up-to-date technical facilities.

A monument to A. S. Griboyedov (sculptor V. V. Lishev) has been erected in front of the theatre. The poet is shown sitting in deep reflection: the expression on his face is thoughtful and faintly mocking.

Other new works of monumental sculpture which appeared in the last few years must be mentioned here. One is the monument to Mikhail Kalinin, a prominent figure in the Communist Party and the Soviet Government, installed in the centre of the square in front of the Gigant Cinema (sculptor M. G. Manizer). Also in Vyborg Side, a monument has been erected to A. A. Kondratyev, a hero of the Civil War and one of the first Komsomol members, after whom a street in this industrial district has been named. This monument was designed by G. D. Glikman. Then in Kirovsky Prospekt there is the statue of A. S. Popov, the Russian scientist who invented the radio, (sculptor V. Y. Bogolyubov). A monument to N. A. Dobrolyubov, cast from a model by V. A. Sinaisky, has appeared at the intersection of

Bolshoi Prospekt and Oleg Koshevoi Street in Petrograd Storona. A bust of Nadezhda Konstantinovna Krupskaya has been set up in Obukhovskaya Oborona Prospekt; a monument to the Young Guard of Krasnodon in the Thirtieth Anniversary of the Komsomol Park near the Narva Gates; a bust of F. I. Shubin in the Mikhailovsky Garden; a monument to the heroes of the Oktyabrsky district division of the People's Volunteers in Sadovaya Street; and a monument to Young Pioneer heroes in the Tavrichesky Garden.

On May 9, 1960, the 15th anniversary of victory over nazi Germany, a monument to the citizens and defenders of Leningrad who died or were killed in the war was unveiled at the Piskarevsky Memorial Cemetery where the common graves are. A whole memorial ensemble has been designed by architects Y. A. Levinson and A. V. Vasilyev. A streight path, paved with concrete slabs, leads from the gate to the centre of the monument dominated by the figure of a woman personifying Motherland (sculptors V. V. Isayeva and R. K. Taurit). Behind the monument is a wall with bas-reliefs dedicated to the memory of the dead. The inscription on this monument begins with the words of the poetess Olga Bergholtz: "Here lie Leningraders. Here lie its citizens—men, women and children. Beside them lie Red Army soldiers. They defended you with their lives, Leningrad . . . ." And it ends with the words: "Looking at these stones, remember: no one has been forgotten, nothing has been forgotten."

Documentary materials about Leningrad in the Great Patriotic War have been collected and deposited in the two pavilions on either side of the gate.

The majestic composition in the Piskarevsky Cemetery is a memorial of eternal glory to those thousands and thousands of heroes who had defended the city from enemy invasion in the grim years of war.

Another memorial to the defenders of Leningrad has been erected in the Serafimovsky cemetery (sculptor Y. N. Lukin). It was unveiled on January 27, 1965, on the 21st anniversary of the day when the nazis were completely routed near Leningrad. The monument is stern and laconic. A sailor, an old worker, a woman, a young worker and a soldier, personifying the defenders of Leningrad, stand with bowed heads before the graves of the fallen. Grey granite pylons make the background for these

Memorial in Serafimovsky Cemetery

TV centre

figures which were designed by a group of young sculptors, headed by R. K. Taurit.

More monuments to the defenders of Leningrad, for which thousands of people everywhere in the Soviet Union have donated money, will be erected in the nearest future.

Monuments to Lomonosov, Gogol, Mendeleyev and other prominent figures in Russian science and culture are also planned. The foundation stone for a monument to Lenin has already been laid in front of the Moscow Station—the main gateway to the town.

Several large public buildings were completed in the jubilee year, 1967. One was the Oktyabrsky concert hall, the largest in the city, designed by architects V. A. Kamensky, A. V. Zhuk, Zh. M. Verzhbitsky and G. M. Vlanin, in Ligovsky Prospekt, near Moscow Railway Station. Another was the Sovietskaya Hotel in Lermontovsky Prospekt, at the crossing with the Fontanka, built by architects Y. A. Levinson, V. V. Gankevich, A. I. Pribulsky. The main building is nineteen storeys high with another five-storey building adjoining it. There are altogether 1,100 rooms which can accommodate approximately 1,400 guests. The third is the Yubileiny (Jubilee) Palace of Sports (architects I. P. Suslikov and G. P. Morosov) with a cylindrical main building, 90 m. in diameter, which can seat more than 7,000 spectators watching ice hockey, basketball, volleyball games, boxing matches, etc.

Quite a number of public buildings have appeared in the last few years, among them the Vyborg, Druzhba, Zarya and Kiev Hotels, the Vostok Restaurant in Victory Park, the motoring station near the Obvodny Canal, and the television centre—one of the largest in Europe—in Chapygin Street on Petrograd Side (architects S. Speransky, A. Katz and V. Vasilkovsky). The television tower on the banks of Bolshaya Nevka is 316 metres high—16 metres higher than the Eiffel Tower. More than 250 concrete piles had to be driven deep into the ground to provide the tower with a reliable foundation.

Housing development is going on apace. And although we are used to the rate of development of the past fifty years, still the scale on which the work has been launched in our day, in the late nineteen-sixties, is astonishing. Suffice it to say that more than 50,000 new flats are tenanted every year.

This means an annual increment of 1,600,000 sq.m. of dwelling space, which will be all the more impressive if we remember that in 1917 the city's entire dwelling space equalled 16,000,000 sq.m.

The bulk of the new apartment houses is built in the large industrial districts of Leningrad and the outskirts. As a rule, standard designs are used, and building is done according to modern industrial methods. The new neighbourhoods in Novo-Izmailovsky Prospekt, Avtovo, Dachnoye and Shchemilovka give a good idea of the scale of housing development.

Under the general plan of development, the existing number of flats will be almost doubled in 1980. Construction will mainly continue in the southern and northern parts of town, and adjoining districts will be merged.

The task of constructing a sea front for Leningrad will also be solved. As mentioned earlier, a beginning was made by building the Kirov Stadium on the shore of the Gulf of Finland. Eventually, a five-metre-long boulevard will run along the embankment, fronted by multi-storey houses. A large Primorsky Park has been laid out on the southern shore of the Gulf of Finland, and new residential districts will grow up beside it. The northern shore, between Novaya Derevnya and Lakhta, will also be built up. Thus, the "sea front" will embrace the mouth of the Neva and the shores of the Gulf.

A park zone, ten to fifteen kilometres wide, is being planted round Leningrad. It will make a good place for outings, and the air in the city will be all the purer for it.

Leningrad is beautiful in any weather, in any season: in winter when its monuments and wrought-iron grilles are covered with rime, in spring when gleaming sheets of broken ice rush down the Neva, in summer when the gardens are carpeted with green grass, and in autumn when the falling yellow leaves settle on the still waters of the rivers, canals and ponds. But, probably, Leningrad is most beautiful in the season of white nights in June. Go out in the hour before sunrise and look at the panorama sung by so many poets—the majestic flow of the Neva with the raised bridges suspended above the water, the golden spires glimmering in the distance, the perspective of the straight, wide streets, the wast, slumbering squares, and the clearly etched silhouettes of monuments and grilles. The memory will remain with you always.

. . . It's almost morning. A cool, fresh breeze is blowing from the Gulf. The line of sky behind the fanciful domes of the Smolny Nunnery is paling. The first pedestrians appear in the streets. The ships on the river give their sad, drawn-out signals. Trams, buses and trolleybuses start out from their depots in an endless stream. The first metro train arrives at the underground passenger platform. A new working day begins in Leningrad, the hero-city.

Moskovsky Prospekt

REQUEST TO READERS

Progress Publishers would be glad to have your opinion of this book, its translation and design and any suggestions you may have for future publications.

Please send your comments to 21, Zubovsky Boulevard, Moscow, USSR.

Редактор русского текста
Л. П. Чернова

Художественный редактор
Ю. В. Самсонов

Технический редактор
Г. Н. Калинцева

Подписано к печати 30/I 1973 г.
Формат 60 × 74 1/16.
Бум. л. 10 5/8. Печ. л. 17,43. Уч.-изд. л. 18,49.
Издат. № 11133. Цена 4 р. 71 к.

Издательство «Прогресс»
Государственного комитета
Совета Министров СССР
по делам издательств,
полиграфии и книжной торговли
Москва Г-21, Зубовский бульвар, 21

Изготовлено в ГДР

DATE DUE